To Octavia
Keep the ...

Don't Shoot the Messenger

~ *The Teachings of an Ancient Chinese Master* ~

Love

Introduction by Alan Whitehead
Edited by Sasi Langford

www.dontshootthemessenger.co.uk

Dedicated to the memory of my dear friend

SUSIE MUELLER

1952 – 1998

A truly enlightened soul who loved me unconditionally and changed the way I thought about everything, without ever wanting to change me.

Alan Whitehead
Summer, 2014
Bragbury End
Hertfordshire

ACKNOWLEDGEMENTS

Without the help and encouragement of Bryan and Sasi this book would never have become a reality.

I have known Bryan since 1978 and together we have experienced 'The Dream', laughing and joking our way through countless travels and retreats. His help getting this book 'right' has been ongoing and we have talked every day about love, life, the universe, the futility of Man's stupidity and attempting to make some sense of it all.

Not sure if we're making any progress, but none of it matters anyway. He has been a true friend and my constant confidante through the ups and downs of life.

Sasi, as clever as she is beautiful, has been inspirational in writing this book in a form that is readable, yet true to the original transcripts. There seems to be nothing she can't do, glass of wine in one hand and a roll up ciggie in the other. An absolute pleasure to be with, work with, laugh with.

On advertising for a copy writer, the minute I spoke to her on the phone I knew she was 'the one'. As soon as we meet, I felt a past life connection. Her contribution to this book has been invaluable…a delight to know in every way.

CONTENTS

INTRODUCTION

I have to say that this life, using the body known as Alan Whitehead, has been an interesting journey – some people might even say exciting.

Rock star, music manager and strip club owner – I have definitely 'done' life, big time. Experiencing fame and fortune, a path which I chose for my soul's growth, has helped me understand that the material world has nothing to offer in the long term (although it's been a lot of fun).

Born in July, a typical Leo, this life has been a roller coaster of a ride, with no sign of it slowing down, or me getting off any time soon, at the tender age of 69.

My motto has always been "Live every day as if it's your last, because one day it will be". This attitude to life has served me well, and I have always been open to changes.

I met Susie Mueller in 1973, a yoga teacher from California (bear in mind that yoga was still considered very 'alternative', if not downright weird, in those days), at the height of fame as drummer with The Marmalade pop group. This was a meeting of old souls, a contract made in a former life, and I knew immediately that I had been destined to meet her, to facilitate the extraordinary changes to my consciousness. Susie loved me unconditionally, and it was her patience and love that helped me discover myself by introducing me to The Circle for Inner Truth, and the remarkable teachings of Chung Fu.

We met every week in an old church hall in Holland Park, West London, only about 20-30 of us, all eager for change and answers about the purpose of our lives.

Chung Fu was kind and gentle with us, never judgemental, and always patient with our naïve, (sometimes stupid) questions, much like a grandfather with his grandchildren. Many of Chung Fu's teachings resonate deeply in a world that is even more stressed out and confused than when these lessons were first expressed through The Vehicle (Marshall Lever), so now seems to be a good time for his guidance to be shared with a new generation of students in the 'University of Life'.

I'm only the Messenger, but I hope the beauty and understanding of Chung Fu's teachings will help you find some of the answers you seek.

Blessings and Peace...and may the Living Spirit within bring you peace.

A.W.
September, 2014

EDITOR'S NOTE

When I heard that Alan was looking for someone to help with a book project I assumed, as did many others, it was going to be his rock and roll memoirs. I couldn't have been more surprised when the true nature of his project was revealed.

At our first meeting, the ever-effervescent Al, his eyes sparkling, presented me with a stack of old photocopied paper. These were transcripts of original audio tapes from several trance channelling sessions, many of which he had attended in London during the early 1970's. I visualised that chilly Holland Park hall in 1974, and saw his younger self amidst a glorious sea of emerald-green crocheted maxi dresses, paisley shirts and purple flares. I heard the scrape of chairs echoing around the room as they entered and took their seats, and caught a whiff of incense and patchouli in the air. An overwhelming sense of anticipation permeated the atmosphere as these enquiring minds, hoping to embark on a new journey, turned their eager faces and watched intently as Marshall Lever – The Vehicle – fell into his trance.

Al explained how this small hand-picked audience was arranged in a pyramid formation, with its apex closest to

The Vehicle, gradually widening out in longer rows of chairs further away from the dais. The strength of the pyramid shape would bolster the energies being channelled which, while not dangerous, always took its toll physically on The Vehicle.

As the weeks progressed, Al recalled more and more details of the sessions – that The Vehicle always had a towel draped over his left arm, strategically placed to catch the saliva that often dribbled out as his head lolled before Chung Fu appeared, and the extreme frailty with which Marshall emerged from his trance after each lesson, drained and exiting the hall as quickly as his exhausted state allowed, to avoid questions that he couldn't possibly answer.

While it was relatively easy to imagine the scene, the real challenge was to turn these transcripts – full of repetitions, inaudible mumbles and sometimes incomprehensible grammar – into lucid text that would be understood by a new 21st century audience, whilst still retaining the essence of Chung Fu's message, with as little alteration to the original text as possible.

Under Alan and Bryan's watchful eye, unnecessarily ornamental terms such as 'personages' and 'within' were replaced by 'people' and 'in' where appropriate. We have cut excessive verbal repetition from the transcripts to make it flow more easily for the reader, but because we present the lessons in chronological order the reader might notice some minor duplication of content across various chapters. Here, again, we wanted to avoid a major dissection of the original content.

We also debated more weighty issues, such as Chung Fu's choice of words when referring to 'mongoloid' children (we agreed to use Down Syndrome but have also inferred that Chung Fu might be referring to other types of cognitive or physical disabilities), or his assertion that no vegetable contains the same amount of nutrients as an animal source of protein (given that genetically modified super-foods were not prevalent at the time, and that certain fish has higher levels of B12 than beef).

From my own perspective, the last few months have irreversibly broadened my horizons. I am delighted that Al and Bryan chose me out of dozens of hopeful editors and copy-writers, placing their faith in me so completely, giving me nothing but encouragement and support at every stage of preparing this book.

Absorbing and making sense of Chung Fu's words was a fascinating experience, but by far the greatest pleasure has been working with two of the most compassionate, fun-loving and kindest human beings I have met in this lifetime. I shouldn't really have been surprised, though. After all, as they both said, with supreme conviction in our preliminary editorial meeting, "Open up to the Universe, Sasi, and the Universe will open up to you".

Sasi Langford
London
September, 2014

INTRODUCTION TO

A CIRCLE FOR INNER TRUTH

A Circle for Inner Truth was formed to help man broaden his spiritual perspectives. The founders' concept is that man's spirit is immortal, that man has a series of existences on Earth through reincarnation, and that the spirit existed prior to being embodied in man on Earth, and will continue in existence subsequent to being embodied in man on Earth. The founders believe the spirit represents a God Force and is located within man, and to break the cycle of reincarnation on earth, man must identify with the God Force within himself during an Earth cycle. This identification is a spiritual realization that man is the God Force within. After this realization, man is spiritually immortal, eternal and universal.

A Circle for Inner Truth is centred on the teachings and guidance of Chung Fu, the spirit guide of trance medium Marshal N. Lever. Chung Fu is the assumed name of the spirit guide has chosen from the I-Ching meaning Inner Truth. Chung Fu works with a spirit group through his medium, and he has stated that his last reincarnation was as a student of Lao-Tzu, in China. Chung Fu communicates through his medium in semi-trance and in full trance and only when the medium's wife, Quinta Joy Lever, has her supportive vibration present. Personal readings are done in semi-trance. All spiritual teaching is done in groups in semi-trance or in full trance.

Personal readings or spiritual counselling centres on the needs of the individual. The guide will consider on all needs, but specializes in health and nutrition, individual spiritual growth and intra-personal relationships. The guide will work with past-life relationships only when it will allow the individual to grow.

Spiritual teachings are given by the guide in full trance and only in groups. When speaking through his medium, his voice is of Chinese accent, his gestures show oriental rhythm and charm, and his dialogue is filled with old Chinese sayings and analogies.

Healing is done through individual readings and is 'cause' healing only. Cause healing shows the individual what caused the difficulty in his body and how to work to alleviate the problem himself. Centering on the cause allows the individual to see himself genetically, psychologically, physiologically and spiritually. Chung

Fu says, "There are no incurable diseases in your world, just incurable people."

Mail readings are almost like personal readings but are done once each week, in absence of the person, and recorded on tape and sent to the individual.

Marshall and Quinta Lever graduated from the University of Arizona, and have made A Circle for Inner Truth their way of life. They have travelled throughout the world with their work and make their home base in San Francisco. They have two children who travel with them and are a vital part of their work.

Excerpt taken from A Circle For Inner Truth manifesto, c. 1972

~ I am in tune with life, and life is in tune with me ~

DIMENSIONS OF MAN

Fallbrook, California – 2 May 1974

Blessings and peace to you all, and may the Living Spirit come forth in every vibration of you physical world and give you peace.

All too often in your world there are misrepresentations and misunderstandings of what the Living Spirit is: of what it is, where it is going and *why* it is. There are many who proclaim that the Living Spirit is this or is that, but the Living Spirit, or God Force, is in all things. It could be in a truck, or a building or in a statue – it permeates everything in your material world.

Old Chinese has said many times that there has never been a beginning and there will never be an end to the Living Spirit. As you sit here, you are a part of the Infinite, undergoing a never-ending evolution. You have been on this earthly plane approximately nine lifetimes, gradually stepping above the physical plane, encountering opportunities to go into other evolutions and other worlds. After each lifetime, you return to the Spirit World for solidification, renewal and to rework a vibration of the highest purity.

Now, what were you before your existence as Man? What were you before? Were you animal? Some say that you were. Were you, perhaps, a plant? Some say that you were. Were you mineral? Some point to the possibility of that existence also. But what were you *really*?

Your spirit is of the Spirit World, the world of the Higher Self. While your soul works on the earthly plane, experiencing and receiving through the five senses, the spirit connects energy to the soul. This is the link of the Living Spirit, your connection with everything that you have ever been and will ever be. Yet, before those existences, you had others, but how best to describe them and what you actually were?

Most of you were vibration, which in itself, is a much misused word, almost as misused as the word 'Love'. To start our explanation, let us say that everything on the earthly plane is a vibration perceived through Man's five senses. However, before your present incarnation, you experienced other different vibrations, on the physical level.

Tree, plant, rock, flower, animal, insect, Man – all have the Living Spirit within them, but Man is best able to express the Living Spirit, as are animals, but to a lesser extent. Your entire being expresses the living energy within you, whether it be through your cells, your blood, or the atoms and molecules that you are made of.

Nothing in your world is 'dead', apart from the word 'dead'. Even if your body dies, it will return to the earth and become part of it again. Around you, the walls, the floor, ceiling and fixtures all possess vibrations, are alive and part of the Living Spirit. Therefore nothing is truly 'dead' – they have merely become a different vibration. You have vibrations of your own, but also those that you receive through your senses.

Firstly, the vibration of touch. If you touch a pine tree or an oak, you will feel its hardness and strength. Whether you touch the soft blossom of a plum tree or feel the sharp sting of a nettle, these are vibrations. The combinations that make up any living thing, be it a tree or a single-cell organism, are all living and creating vibrations. The oak tree has a vibration of touch that you can sense, for you are physically oriented, but it also has an intangible vibration.

Taste is also a vibration, a little more refined than touch, and very closely aligned with smell. The vibration of burning rice or the aroma of spring blossom are vibrations that you can taste and smell, perceived through the air.

What do you see? Colour, the reflection of light, originates from white light. In total darkness, there will be no colour because you have colour only as light reflects upon it, and so colour is also a vibration. From the vibration of red, which is very low, to the violet vibration which is very high, these are vibrations that can be perceived only when light reflects these vibrations.

Then we have sound, whether it is a harmonic beat or rhythm, or a loud explosion, sound is a vibration, higher than that of colour. Sometimes sound is so loud you can feel it, other times so highly tuned that you cannot hear it.

These are all vibrations, and each of you, through various reincarnation cycles, have experienced and existed as these vibrations of touch, taste, colour, sound and smell. All these vibrations contain the God Force, another dimension, another world, that exists besides yours, and in the evolutions that that you have experienced before the one you are now.

You are a combination of not only these previous evolutions, but of all life, expressing the God Force in a different way. When you yourselves were vibrations, the Living Spirit was expressed that way, but now you are experiencing it through physicality, creativity and the existence you are living. After this earthly plane you will have other states of existence that will make this existence seem very small. This is a part of the journey, only a stepping stone.

But at the same time, there are many evolutions going on in this world, side by side with you: the evolution of a plant, or a flower, or a tree, a rock or a gemstone, or an animal. All of these have a vibration, a smell, a taste and a touch that expresses the Living Spirit that is vital to their evolution.

However, because Man is the highest physical evolution on this plane, the Mineral, Animal and Plant Kingdoms respond and evolve only through his love and attention. As your body will one day return to the earth, it will renew and evolve, for the Living Spirit is in mineral and water. Your Higher Self, which is the culmination of many lifetimes, will not evolve without the love of Self.

Of the four elements – Earth, Air, Fire and Water – Man is responsible for three of these. His love and respect for Earth, Air and Water will help him evolve, but lack of attention to these elements means Man must wait much longer to evolve.

The element of Fire, as embodied in the Sun, is of a higher evolution than Man, far beyond your understanding, but one that your world is reliant on. You have other planets in the furthest reaches of your solar system that have earth, air and water, yet they still have no life. They need Fire, the Sun, to bring life from the darkness and cold.

The Sun, and the light it produces, is a physical representation of the Living Spirit on your plane. Whenever Old Chinese is with you, there is a light of Fire, the physical representation of the God Force. Old Chinese uses the vibration of a lifetime 2,400 years ago. He cannot use the vibration of his Higher Self that was created after leaving the earthly plane, for that would destabilize your plane. In order to teach from that Higher Self, Old Chinese uses the vibration of his last earthly existence.

There is nothing that Man creates that is not made from plants or the earth. Whether it is a door handle or a nail hammered into a piece of wood, Livingness exists within everything. Evolution only takes place in the vibration of a purer form, and Man is responsible for only those things that are important for *his* evolution on this plane.

So you see, we are dealing with many evolutions and you are not the only one. You are not the centre of the Universe, even though you contain the Living Spirit. Understanding this, by loving yourself and every breath, vibration and every ounce of energy that you possess, enables you to express a power that is beyond any of the other evolutions on your plane, with the exception of fire.

Some of your religions say that the next great destruction or Cataclysm will be by fire. Does this mean a burning fire, or the element of fire? What can renew polluted water? Fire can renew that water. Polluted earth? Fire can cleanse and renew the earth. Fire is a pure and purifying essence.

You may have heard of other planes existing in parallel to yours. Places such as Venus and Mars, and you may wonder if there is life on these planets. Yes, there is, but life that you cannot see, in another evolution, another dimension.

And so you say, "Where is this all going? I feel so insignificant, so small, like a tiny pin." Consider the pin. Smallness is not a question of actual size, it is about the amount of God Force you allow to come through. You can be the Universe within yourself or let the Universe overwhelm you. You can be every evolution you have ever been, or be nothing at all. The abilities you have both to absorb and express through touch, taste, smell, hearing or sight, are infinite, for they relate not only to the physical aspect, but through clairsentience of the intangible web to the heart, the clairvoyance of the etheric web to the eye, the clairaudience of the etheric web to the ear and throat, and the entire etheric web to the mind which is a combination of all the above.

When you have unlocked your Higher Forces and can communicate beyond the physical plane into the spiritual, you will return to your Higher Self and add this current experience to it. The Higher Self is your home, a place where your soul rests as you evolve through eternity and all those who have lived before will recognize and understand it. But the Living Spirit needs constant expression. The more Living Spirit is expressed, the more Living Spirit is created. You can love yourself, but if you do not express the Living Spirit you will not be lovable. Thusly, central to the expression of the Livingness of things, in the community of all life forms that are evolving, is love of the Living Spirit.

Where are you now? Are you worried about tomorrow or about today? Are you concerned with the future or with yesterday or are you more worried about the thousands of parts inside your body evolving? Remember that you are responsible for many more evolutions other than your own. Do not hesitate to be awed by this, for if you do not understand this, then you will have to wait until you evolve toward that understanding.

Blessings and peace, you may ask your questions.

Q: What will we be next? Do we always start our new cycle with some sort of disability?

OC: All too often we want to see what lies over the hill and if we do not see the flowers, trees and butterflies here, when we get over the hill we won't see the flowers , trees and butterflies there. You will not be deficient, for that is of another plane. You are dealing with a different evolution and to enter it you must not care what it is, as long as you can enter in. Peace.

Q: Would entering the next plane as a severely disabled child be easier than some of the other next lives that we might enter? Would that be a slower way of evolving?

OC: You are not going to reach the last existence of that evolution, that much we can guarantee. It will be slow. Peace.

Q: I heard that a long time ago, Zoroastrianism worshiped the spirit in fire. Could you talk a little on that?

OC: Zoroaster was a master, a least Old Chinese and the Brotherhood he works with consider him a master. They worshipped the spirit and power of the vibration of the sun and the stars, and fire's physical form as embodied by the salamander. They believed the moon was a reflection of all this fire and that the sun actually created the three primary colours – the red of the sun, the yellow of its rays and blue, the colour created as it travels to Earth through the ether. Fire is a highly evolved natural element, the essence of which was revered by the Zoroastrians. By understanding its nature they centred on the spiritual fire that was within themselves, not the flame of a candle or a burning tree. The warmth that lies in Man's soul, the Eternal Fire that lies at the core of oneself. It was during an argument about the worship of fire that Zoroaster died by a spear through his stomach. Peace.

Q: Dear spiritual brother, can you give us some guidance on how to establish a constructive, harmonious relationship with the pocket gophers, mice, ants and things of thing nature?

OC: What is a…pocket gopher?

Q: (laughter) It is a small animal…a pest.

OC: Let me visualize (pause) Rodent…Old Chinese sees. First you must know that when ants bother you, they want your food, so why not feed them, outside your pagoda. If you see ants, take some honey and put it outside, and thus you won't have them inside. If you are in harmony with all living things, and do not eat the flesh of living things, you will find that the pocket rodent will not offend you because you will be in harmony with them. When you are in harmony with your Higher Self even the mosquito will not bite you. That sounds unbelievable, but it is true. Even the fly will not bother you. By respecting all living things and understanding they are all linked on an evolutionary plane, they will seek refuge in your understanding.

If you have an imbalance in a biological sense, it is you who has created it. An animal can eat gopher, rodent or ants. Insects eat ants, but if you killed these creatures then you have not honoured them. If you have peace within yourself and step above, you will find that they do not disturb you. Even if they take food from your hand, you will feel that they are as one with you. All too often chemical death is a result of biological and mental imbalance. Consider things as they grow. There is always enough fruit or fruit from animals to nourish Man's existence. Do not worry about their evolution, for by giving them your love and attention, you and they will evolve. Peace.

Q: Chung Fu, we have a problem in this area with cats killing the birds. Is it our place to protect the birds or is this the evolution of the cat?

OC: Why do they kill birds in your area? Because you feed them in your area, do you not? Wherever you are

32

creating an imbalance in nature, when you feed a cat or a bird, they become reliant on you. They receive love from you, so you then bear the responsibility to prevent the bird's death. This isn't done by killing the cat, but by greater diligence. Sometimes a cat's evolutionary path involves a bird or rodent, and you have no responsibility there. Your love of the cat will help it evolve, and your love for the birds help them evolve and it is possible to raise cats and birds side by side.

When a bird is pulled to you, away from their natural feeding grounds they will be susceptible to new dangers. They will become centred on your love and feel that any movement in your garden is essentially friendly. A bird in the wild does not have to worry about a cat, they have other natural predators that they are tuned in to. If a cat catches a bird it is an evolutionary process, but one in which you take responsibility. You should not condone the death of a bird, but at the same time you cannot control it. It seems that as Man and animals live closer together there is more death.

So, when the cat gets the bird, know that you are not entirely responsible, but remember the bird has become dependent on you. It is a fine line, Old Chinese knows, for often you feed the birds for a period of time, then leave and the bird will not know what to do and will starve. If you can love a cat and feed a bird consistently, the way it meets its death, as long as it is not directly by your hand, you are not responsible. By consistently loving both entities there will eventually be an understanding. Peace.

Q: Chung Fu, 17% of the world's population follow Islam. From your plane, what do you think of Mohammed?

OC: This religion was founded at a time when there was great turmoil and great need in your world. You, at one time, were also Islam. It is an evolutionary process even though it is a religion, and in a way, it allows one to focus on the God Force, but it is used for their own gains, it is true. However, by giving these people a spiritual focus, they find a stepping stone to the next plane. Mohammed was a man who had an idea and conveyed it in a time when Christianity had not extended to that part of the world. He actually endorsed and taught many of the Nazarene's philosophies.

Consider the death and scourges in the Old Testament, where battles were waged in the name of God. You cannot point the finger solely at Mohammedism for such aggression. Both the Nazarene and Mohammed taught peace, but their followers taught war. How many wars have been waged in the name of the Nazarene? How many people have died so that Christianity might live? It is not the master as much as his followers who have created wars for their own benefit. Peace.

Q: Chung Fu, is it the evolution of animals like seals and whales to be killed by Man? You say not to judge, but if it isn't their evolution, who is supposed to help them?

OC: Remember that an animal has a group soul and cannot evolve without the love of Man. If Man kills an animal, it is his responsibility and his karma, not the whale's. The group soul of seal or whale can evolve through such events, but spiritually, if you love an individual whale or seal then you are responsible for its evolution until its body dies. The question is, are you ready for that responsibility? Peace.

Q: I read that some people think it's just as bad to eat plants as it is animals because plants are also alive. What are your thoughts on that?

OC: When you eat fruit, does it kill the plant? When you eat a nut, does it kill the plant? Take a berry from the bush or a melon from the vine and the plant lives on. You should not eat potato, unless the potato is a certain potato, which Old Chinese cannot pronounce because it has two letters together than are most difficult. The plant dies before the potato is harvested, and you should not eat things that kill the plant. There are many such fruits and plants that are available to you. If you take a banana the tree does not die, or if you cut asparagus, the asparagus will continue to grow for seven years. If you harvest a lettuce, then you have killed it, but carefully peel its leaves while it is in the garden and it will live for at least five years. Peace.

Q: Chung Fu, is it right to take plants out of their natural environments?

OC: First of all, what now would you call 'natural', as your world contains so much 'unnaturalness' these days? Think in terms of biological imbalance – if a plant is taken from one part of the world and brought here it may grow, but the bugs here may kill it, or the bird that kills the bug is not here. In that way yes, but in another way, no. You can create a vibration between you and them that will allow the foreign plant to live and the bugs will not kill it. But there are not many of those, maybe two places in your world. Peace.

Q: Can you say something about Jehovah's Witnesses? We have a good friend who is one and it's hard for us to communicate because we believe in the Living Spirit and they don't.

OC: If you cannot communicate, then it is not their problem, it is yours. Each person is in evolution whether they are of one religion or one fear. Whether they are an aborigine in a far-off land, a highly evolved Master or they live in fundamental fear, that is their evolution, and important for their growth. Let them grow in their own way, and do not infringe on their way of growth, even if they infringe upon yours. Do not try to combat and defend what you think, for defence of your point of view essentially means that you do not truly believe in it. If it is the truth that you are living, it does not need defending, and if it is not the truth, then it is not worth defending.

Remember that they are where they need to be and you are where you need to be, all part of the stairway, none higher than another because if it wasn't for the step beneath you wouldn't have reached where you are now. So when others try to push their beliefs on you, listen, but do not engage them in combat, or say anything bad, for that is what they want. Live your belief, live what you think. Don't talk it, express it through clairsentience that any religion would feel comfortable with. Peace.

Q: Chung Fu, you say the Living Spirit has no beginning and no end. Is that the same for us too?

OC: The Living Spirit could not create itself and the same applies same to you. What does it feel like to realize that you are eternal, immortal and universal? For that is what you are. Do not worry about the future, for you have eternity to live in. Peace.

Q: Why do we live the lives that we live if we are a part of the Living Spirit to begin with? When did we start our incarnations?

OC: They were never started, they have always been. Let us look at it this way: You love the Living Spirit by loving

Self. Sometimes you cannot love someone else. If you love the Living Spirit within yourself, you automatically love the Living Spirit within them because it is the same in them as it is in you. But if, when you look at their personality, you cannot see the expression of Living Spirit within them, you will not be drawn to them. Each lifetime is full of that expression and you are learning to express it through more than just the physical. The next existence will become progressively brighter as you go into Infinity. You will express the Living Spirit in an energy and power that will make a lightning bolt seem like a mere flicker in the dark. You must express your growing power in slow steps, allowing the Living Spirit to come through your body and evolve out of this earth plane, ready for the next existence. The more light you express the more light there will be. You are concerned with the physical body's evolution, but your spirit is a higher part and is a consistent expression of an energy that is beyond your current understanding. It is there, and each incarnation or evolution you are contains the Living Spirit, and so the Living Spirit *is* you. Peace.

Q: Chung Fu, what is the God Force?

OC: The same as the Living Spirit. Two terms Old Chinese has used. Peace.

Q: Chung Fu, I would be grateful if you would touch on forgiveness of sins as taught in the orthodox Christian churches, particularly in relation to karma.

OC: At no time was it taught by the Nazarene. Even the book of Mark, which is the only sound book in in the New Testament, contains some misinterpretations. The Book of Mark was written in 55 A.D., Matthew in 120 A.D., Luke in 90 A.D., and John in 70 A.D. when you leave this place tonight, some of you will retell what Old Chinese has said, but it will be different to what Old Chinese has *actually* said. Many things that are attributed to the Nazarene, he did not say. That is important to remember. The forgiveness of sins is a creation of the priesthood to make Man reliant on them and not themselves, for if you have sins to be forgiven then you have to turn to priests. It was decided that reincarnation would no long be accepted in the Christian faith for it did not allow priests or the church to have power over Man. If Man no longer had to worry, because he understood that his life was simply an evolutionary process through which he would evolve to another life, what role could the priests play? Such beliefs were eliminated by religious law.

And so, the forgiveness of sins does not exist as you cannot show me one sin in your world. If you say killing someone is a sin, on whose shoulders does the sin rest? The person you killed is as responsible, if not more so, than the person that killed them, because they drew it to themselves. Whether you are an alcoholic in the gutter or an alcoholic walking with your head held high, teaching others how to deal with alcoholism, that is the path of your effect pattern. Those who come into this world to experience alcoholism can let their effect pattern drive them to the gutter or they can work with it with beauty and help others overcome it. This is the same principle as the forgiveness of sins, for there are no sins to be forgiven. You have never made a mistake because there *are* no mistakes. They are experiences, and as you evolve and see these things you will see the God Force at work. The recognition of sin is a physical factor that says you do not recognize the Living Spirit and pushes it into the background. Peace.

~ ~ ~ ~ ~ ~ ~ ~ ~

In Old China, long ago, a sage sat under a plum tree. A student approached and said, "Where should I go to find peace?" The sage replied, "What peace are you looking for?" The student said, "Peace from all the corners of this world. Peace from the emperor's raids on our region. Peace from money worries and from lack of food. I want to have that kind of peace." The sage said, "Sit with me under this tree and you will find peace." The student sat and after five days the student said to the sage, "It is peaceful here. You have freedom from all the earthly things because you have placed yourself above them, but I find it boring." The sage said, "What is boring?" The student replied, "I have nothing to do." The sage said, "Then go out into your world until you are ready for peace within, for peace can only be there when you step back and watch the world go by, not when you are involved within it. But by watching it go by you *are* within it. For you know when to associate and because of the peace that you have, those that need peace will also stop at your plum tree."

May your plum tree be as peaceful as you wish it to be. Blessings and Peace to you all.

~ When I am right on the inside, everything is right on the outside ~

NEGATIVITY

Fallbrook, California – 16 May 1974

Blessings and Peace to you all and may the God Force in all living things come forth and give each of you peace within and understanding beyond your understanding. Blessings and Peace.

We have often taught of the Living Spirit, the Livingness of all things, in this university of the physical plane. There are no dead things in your world, for nothing truly dies because everything contains Livingness. The vibrations of all things, of walls and floors, of rock and stone, all contain the God Force within them. Old Chinese hopes you will come to recognise that you are the combination of many living elements that makes up the God Force, and the way you express the God Force is the way you are.

But your world still does not fully acknowledge the Living Spirit or God Force. Everything around you is aimed at the physical, oriented on your five senses and so many times you are not aware of what you are receiving. There is an exception, and that is peace because peace is a physical state, as well as a spiritual one. From your early childhood you absorb the physical negativity of your earthly plane and make it a part of your life. Why do you think your world is so strongly based on the word 'sin'? Why is your world so caught up in the concept of 'guilt'? Why is the evolution and existence of 'wrong' so apparent in your world? Why do you feel that sin becomes a part of your orientation either morally, sociologically or spiritually? From the time that you were small, how many times you have 'sinned' in someone else's eyes? Why do you feel that sin was created or became so tainted with negativity? Where did it come from?

When the last cataclysm caused the switching of the Earth's poles and destroyed most of the human population, apart from pockets of 30 or 40 thousand people, the Earth began anew. Those survivors were on a very high spiritual level, in tune with Nature and had been at the right place at the right time. Go back to that time, a time of beauty and vitality, when Man had to start from the beginning, a time when Man knew and understood all.

He possessed the understanding of an ancient and very advanced civilisation, but in the twinkling of an eye, all that remained were his friends, loved ones and his own inner energy. But why did the idea of sin appear? In a time that could have been perfect, when everything had been scraped clean, why did sin return? And here you are again, 7,000 years later again steeped in sin and guilt. How do you think it began?

Let us use this room as an example. Imagine that everyone here has been fortunate enough to be in a colony that has survived the next cataclysm. You understand the Earth, and knowing what you do *not* want, begin to create a new world, producing the next generation, and you start teaching your children. You have the opportunity to lay the foundations for a brand new world. What do you teach them? What about what you have learned in reading, writing and putting together numbers? Should they learn that? You emerge in a blaze of new living things and so you begin to teach what you value and your child responds to your teaching.

But what of your neighbour who says, "I want my child to learn of the science and technology we had in the Old World, for they will help him understand the power he has." Others will respond, "But that power is what caused the Cataclysm." And so the first hint of 'wrong' appears. The mathematical aspect of your world allows you to understand some vibrations, but if you are at a new beginning, what will mathematics show you? If someone starts to teach incorrectly or differently to what is accepted, then the notion of 'wrong' is formed. Others might say that what you are doing is not in the best interests of the community, because they don't want to teach what was learned before, instead wanting to teach new ideas about life. Then they say to the person who wants to teach the mathematics and science of old: Go. They must leave because the community cannot accept a different vibration amongst them, and that difference becomes sin.

Remember that the God Force is in all living things. It is a manifestation of all energy in your world, but your world says that you sin and by taking your God's name in vain that you commit sin. Old Chinese has never really understood that saying, even in the Hebrew tradition, for if you want to call yourself names, go ahead, for God is within you, not on a mountain top. The Ten Commandments were created to regulate people and control the God Force within, during a time of chaos, laid down by an older generation, but that were questioned by later generations.

You become involved in negativity around you if you find positivity hard to assume – and it is – because you reincarnate into an essentially negative physical world. It is easier to be negative than positive, as it takes energy and creativity to be positive. One of the most destructive feelings is guilt. If you feel guilty about something you did, it is like saying you are sorry you put your left leg on your path before your right one. There is nobody in this room that can tell me something they should feel guilty about. Guilt is a creation of your earth plane to embody power in a physical way. If you transgress the rules and regulations of a religion you feel guilty, and those in charge make you feel guilty also. But perhaps the very fact that you went against it shows its weakness.

When Lao-Tzu, the Nazarene, Buddha and Confucius taught, they said that you could find the Living Spirit or the Creator within yourself, not without, or by adhering to regulations. Why do you think their followers imposed regulations based on the teachings of these Masters after they had departed this earthly plane? If you have Masters of such exceptional vibration, those who remember them will try to retain their teachings, establishing a structure around those teachings.

They will remember that as he walked down the road he was silent and so they will say you must be silent. They will remember when he talked they all sat around and listened, so when they teach they will say all are to listen. They remember the peace he was able to create within, the ability to heal the body. Therefore, they will say if you have a disease it is because you do not believe in him. Regulations are designed to control and that is what happens within any religion, institution or power structure, causing constriction and struggle in your life.

On one side you see disease, poverty, famine, war, and theft, all symptoms of negativity. On the other side you see peace, prosperity and happiness – the signs of positivity, which are always to be found within, not in another world. It is not in heaven, it is the recognition of the Living Spirit. It is understandable why Man becomes confused with these two opposing aspects. From the time you are born, you are subjected to negativity on the earth plane, and it has been this way since the first generation after the

Cataclysm. Remember that disease is a mental creation, an attitude because there are no incurable diseases, only incurable people. Remember that you do nothing wrong, it is only a stage in your evolution and experience pattern.

Peace is the ability to function within restrictions and all of you are restricted. If you say, "I do not feel restricted", get into your automobile and drive on the other side of the road, then drive across someone's lawn and see if you are not restricted. The more physical things you possess, the more restrictions you impose upon yourself, and it is easier to live outside yourself than within. You prefer to journey outward, and have to see everything to believe it, to hear it to know that it is true. You do not believe what is within yourself, nor do you realise that you have the strength to rectify your life. There is no need for great religious teachings or miraculous lightning bolts from above, simply reality and loving yourself. It is that simple. By loving yourself no harm will come to you, you will be in the right place at the right time, and every choice in your life will flow freely. The God Force does not recognise the negativity, prohibition and exorcism that your world is so focused on. The negativity and sins you believe that you commit are only recognised by you.

Your religions say that God is watching you, but *you* are God. However, if you cling to the negative there can be no connection to the God Force. Every day you place restrictions on yourself, when in reality, the God Force can express itself with just a little discipline, not through imposed regulations and figures of authority. It concerns us that we see more and more involvement in the physical world, and we are seeing fewer people stepping off that plane of existence. The more physical awareness you gain, the less spirituality you possess. Science splits the atom – Old Chinese walks through it. Science sends people into outer space – Old Chinese walks from one world to another through a dimensional warp in a matter of seconds, not days.

If someone says that your actions hurt them, your first reaction may be to say that you are sorry. Sorry for what, and who is going to judge that what you have done is wrong? If someone says you have hurt their feelings, what they are really saying is: You have exposed me, and I do not like the truth. You have your reality, they have theirs.

Children adjust and react to their parents' personalities, which is a stage in the re-incarnational cycle. If they are allowed to live their past life within their reincarnation, as they grow older, when someone says to them what you have done is stupid, they will be able to reply: That is only your reality, for what I have done is an experience pattern in my evolution. If you tell a child they are clumsy enough times, they will develop clumsiness in life. Tell them that they are not creative, then they will not be. By never telling them that you love them, through words or actions, they will not love themselves. In their first 12 years a child begins to learn about the God Force by being loved by those who brought them into this world.

In the workplace there are rules and regulations. If someone breaks those rules it is your duty to step in and set them straight. But breaking the rules, or stepping out of line – what is that exactly? A type of responsibility? The word 'responsibility' is much overused in your world. The person who breaks rules in your workplace is not responsible to the organisation, but to themselves. Any employee whose boss has the God Force within will never feel constricted or regulated. Instead, they will feel freedom and work happily.

If the God Force does not recognise negativity, then why be a part of it? Step out beyond it and you will find a new freedom and understanding beyond yourself. If there is only one thing that Old Chinese will teach through the Vehicle it is this: You are the Energy and the Power that you are. What you are, *is*, and what is, you are. Peace.

You may now ask your questions.

Q: In the years after the cataclysm do you think individuals will be released from the negativity of the astral field so that we will more easily recognise out God Self?

OC: If you die in a cataclysm, you will not come back for at least 750 years, more like 1000 years. Only those who are highly spiritually evolved, or very in tune will return. Your astral body is the vibrational Guide of your physical self. When that physical body dies, the soul enters the spirit world and the astral body dissipates. In the spirit world, those who die in a cataclysm will be going to school for many years. It is possible to evolve in the spirit world, but it takes much longer so it is easier and faster to reincarnate here. Peace.

Q: Chung Fu, according to Albert Schweitzer we all need to develop a deep reverence for all life, that we have a kinship with all that is, and all that exists is the Living Spirit. Is this true?

OC: Even the vibration in your world is the Living Spirit, remember your five senses. Colour, touch, sound, smell are all vibrations but perceived differently. Each and everything that you take in has the dimensional vibration of seeing, hearing, touching and tasting. The God Force is vibration too, and what you have said is true. Peace.

Q: We're taught that God is all there is, which is a very general statement. It's hard to perceive and yet I know what you say is true.

OC: Let us look at your body – it is God. Blood, bone, flesh, teeth, hair, all the separate living elements. Your body can be buried for centuries, then exhumed and you can see, using your microscopes, the calcium and magnesium still alive and as strong as it was before death, for calcium does not deteriorate. Thus the God Force is every vibration pulled together. Rocks and plants have a smaller vibrations but they are also an expression of the Living Spirit. The more you pull together the more Living

Spirit and freedom you have on the physical plane. You can even purify your own blood by recognising this. Every movement and vibration is an expression of the God Force, but not through thoughts or the creation of thoughts. In most cases these are manifestations of negativity. Peace.

Q: Could we change our own physical bodies?

OC: You can grow a new arm or leg if it has been severed. It has been done. Do not say anything of this, but the Vehicle has learned through meditation and concentration how to restructure his body through vibration. He had lost half a tooth, but through meditation and faith he replaced it. So can you. Peace.

Q: Chung Fu, do you mean replacing a physical or astral part of the body? What if you lost a part of your physical body?

OC: You could replace it.

Q: Don't some animals have that same facility?

OC: That is true, it is the same vibration on a purer level. Animals have the same abilities in many ways to renew themselves by knowing what to do. Peace.

Q: F. L. Rosen, an Englishman, who studied Science of the Mind, Christian Sciences, gave a beautiful description of the atomic structure of the human body. He says when we align ourselves with our God Force we will have instantaneous healing because the atoms will fall back into the correct position they were at the time prior to birth.

OC: There is some truth here, but you may reincarnate with genetic deficiencies. Through developing a higher understanding and awareness it is possible to create a perfect body, although this is not the important thing, because the Masters teach you to go beyond the physical. However, because the God Force is in all living things, the only thing to heal self, is to love self so powerfully that you know all will be well by lining up your energy and vibrations. Peace.

Q: When the Nazarene performed miracles and cured the sick, was it them believing in themselves that cured them?

OC: The miracles of the Nazarene were not miracles as you think. The blind man saw. What did the blind man see? If the blind man saw the God Force within himself, then he had eyes. It is through cause healing that he learned to heal himself, rather than effect healing when you heal only the wound, not what caused it. The Nazarene not only had the Energy, but he was Cosmic Energy, not a man. When the Nazarene was baptised by John, his soul went to the spirit world, to his higher library. When John pulled him from the baptismal waters the Nazarene's body was filled with cosmic Energy, there was no soul there, but a combination of all living energies. If Cosmic Energy approached you it would not look at you as an individual, it would see God Force and that would be cause healing, for you could heal yourself by recognising yourself in that energy. Peace.

Q: Chung Fu, when the human body dies…

OC: When the soul leaves the body. Continue…

Q: Does cremation or burial affect the Living Spirit in different ways when the soul leaves the body?

OC: You could cremate, homogenise or pasteurise and there would be no loss of the Living Spirit. It is advisable to wait three days before cremation, especially if the deceased is being mourned by unenlightened people. Mourning keeps the soul on the earth level, where it looks for its body but cannot find it. It starts to identify with physical plane or others. Three days gives it time to evolve through our help in the spirit world, but this is not true in all cases as evolved souls will pass over immediately. Cremation is also better because a spirit cannot be earthbound, if the body is cremated. Peace.

Q: Chung Fu, shouldn't the loved ones here on earth recognise the release and be glad they are being released into their Higher Self?

OC: When a soul passes, those who are left should celebrate and let the plum wine flow freely, for it should be a happy moment. Some say it is not, but we know there is never a beginning and never an end. Those who remain usually mourn because they do not know what is within them. Peace.

Q: Chung Fu, please explain to me about twin souls. I realise they're your dual personalities since the beginning.

OC: Dual souls, not twin. You have made us shudder when you say twin souls. You have a spirit library and you have had previous existences in other vibrations before this plane. When you come to this physical experience your librarian or Guide writes two books from the same library. If you reincarnate as a male first, that would have the advantage. So when a new soul comes into the first reincarnation cycle there is also another at the same time but somewhere else. It is a dual experience in the Higher Self whereby one positive and one negative soul are created, each soul having individualistic experiences. For instance you could be the first incarnation of a positive, or as a male, but the next as a woman and the other half.

OC: Blessings and Peace and may the Living Spirit within bring you Peace.

~ My life is filled with happiness, health, abundance and creative self-expression ~

SOLSTICE

London – 21 November 1974

Blessings and Peace to you all on the solstice, this most important time in your world. Know you are the light and the harvest of the summer time, which you have never had before.

In Old China, the emperor built a most beautiful palace. He pulled around him the greatest architects of his world, and brought in stone and marble from all parts of his empire. For 30 years they built this magnificent palace. The emperor went to his wise men and said, "Now I must have a garden to equal the palace." His wise men replied, "There is only one man who can do this. He lies in a province to the south." The emperor sent his men to fetch the esteemed gardener who was brought in before him. The emperor said, "Behold the palace that stands here. It is made from the best stone, the best wood, the best gold, silver and jade. Now I want a garden that will equal that." The gardener replied, "I will need two years," and the emperor said, "So be it."

And so the gardener, an elderly man, built a humble shelter for himself outside the palace. From the summer solstice he sat, watching the birds, watching the rain upon the earth, watching the insects and animals that came and went around the palace. Fall arrived and he watched leaves and clouds change. He watched the coldness of the first frost and pulled his warm cloak more tightly around him. Winter came and he sat in the snow, watching it as it fell, seeing the designs it made around the palace. Spring began and as the frozen waters melted and ran off, the ground created new life as the budding hyacinth heralded the birth of spring.

The summer solstice approached and he began to build his garden. For one year, on each day of every season he gathered and planted more trees and plants. At the end of the next year he asked that the emperor come to see him and said, "Walk with me through your garden."

As they walked and he saw the trees, the gardener said, "When the sun shines through the trees it will make beautiful designs on the ground. When the leaves fall from the trees they will fall into patterns and when the wind blows through the garden they will blow them away and we will never be worried by the leaves. The springs that run through your garden rise and fall, the animals know where to be and the birds fit perfectly within the design. At every full moon the sun and the moon in combination send the reflection of the sun to the moon, thence into your garden. Out of all these trees, if you stand where the moon is behind them, you will see the reflection of one of the symbols of the I-Ching, because the boughs of the trees are made so."

The gardener went on and showed him that in the winter, when the snow fell, it would create beautiful designs beyond the trees. The trees were shaped so that when snow fell, it would look like castles in the air and flying mythical creatures. The gardener turned to the emperor and said, "No matter what day, what hour, what season, for the rest of your life, when you walk from your palace into your garden, it will never be the same. You will never see the same design, the same patterns for it is constructed in eternal growth."

You are the emperor, your Guide is the gardener and the garden is your Higher Self. Old Chinese likewise has an orchard that he cares for, an orchard of which he is the gardener. The plum tree is violet in its fruit and the Chinese plum is known as 'Li', which means 'Eternal Life'. There are many gardens within the physical world, gardens of red and yellow. The fruits of these gardens have Guides also, who enter this world in peace. There have been guardians of the plum orchard before Old Chinese, but now, through the Vehicle's own plum tree, we are tending the orchard at a most crucial time in your world.

During the lifetime of the Vehicle we will reach all of those, in one way or another, who are a part of the plum orchard, for we are the gardeners, pruning and nurturing. Some will bear much fruit, some none at all. Some will have difficulty with disease, but we will always be at the heart of the orchard. Like the emperor, the gardener and the garden, each tree must grow separately, growing within itself and possesses a unique beauty. An orchard is not a community, but a grouping of individuals who are searching for their Higher Selves, their inner gardens.

When Old Chinese left you, not too long ago, he pointed out that he was going to be the gardener, watching the development of those who have been before. Wherever Old Chinese goes, there is much beauty and he sees many people who realize that there are no mistakes or faults, and that certain goals need discipline to achieve, just as the gardener needed discipline to sit in the garden and tend to his plants, or as an athlete needs discipline to shape his body. Without that discipline, your life becomes a flow in no direction. We watch the snow falling, then see the birth of a new spring. In view of all that, Old Chinese, at each equinox and solstice, confers with his higher masters, and reflects on many things.

We have talked many times of an institute, of a centre or community, looking your world over for the correct vibration of that community concept. Of all the places in your world, there were only two. One of these was the vibrational area of the American Indian. Through the love of his eternal self, maintaining peace with the elements and honouring all living things, theirs was a perfect example of devotion to a higher spiritual energy and community. This has been pointed out to Old Chinese by, not only his own Masters, but by Masters that have gone before such as Lao-Tzu, Confucius, the Nazarene and Buddha. In what was once the realm of the native American Indian, not one of their tribes built structures for their communities. These developed long after they had left this earth, with the exception of Pythagoras who built a school, which was eventually destroyed, along with Pythagoras and his wife, because of competing factions within the school.

And so, Old Chinese and those entities that work with him and through him, have decided to create and institute within each of you, to develop the orchard or community within yourself, without controlling the vibration the student has already created themselves. As the gardener or caretaker, we watch the emotions, the feelings of 'belongingness' or inclusivity. This does not lessen the vibration of the student, it will always be there, but our immediate path – by which Old Chinese means three or four hundred years – will be worked within a new medium, creating an institute or garden within yourself. This means not just being taught by Old Chinese, but pulling together strong groups that will help your ability to free flow and create that inner garden, without having to rely on an institute, temple or external community. If you can create an institution within yourself, you do not need a place to withdraw to; there is no need to escape.

Look around you at the churches and places where people meet and talk – you will not need that, you will already have such a place, in your home, in your own self. No Guide or spirit communication in your world is higher than your Higher Self, but they are stepping stones and you must try to build the strongest stepping stones possible.

The Hermetic informs me that since Old Chinese, the Vehicle and Quinta Joy have been in the place you call England, we have communicated through what are known as 'readings' with 2,840 people. As you can see from this, there is great need in your world, but we are not egoistic enough to think that we alone can fill this need. But we must care for our orchard and act as its gardeners. In one way or another, each of you has been instrumental in lighting the spark that is now being fanned to a flickering flame, helping you develop within. Your soul, or your subconscious, is a creation of this lifetime, which you can go beyond, to reach your own inner garden, finding peace within yourself, free from disease and protected from negativity. That is our goal, not a large organisation, not a palatial building, but an intimate space, so that we can always communicate on a personal level. A gardener cannot take care of his garden from within the palace, he must work closely with the flowers and trees.

Many times, we see need and want, feeling what you call 'sadness', but sadness is not really what it appears to be. Although there are many places you may learn from, there is nothing more important than learning within the individual self, focused on creating your own garden, rather than going into someone else's and picking the flowers there.

Some of you are saddened, but in reality, you should be happy because we have given you a chance to be free, and freedom can only exist when seen against restriction. When any Guide says, "This is the end," then that indeed is the end, and because Vehicle has worked with so many since his return, after this night, until the time of Vehicle's birthday, Old Chinese will not come through in full trance. Every time Old Chinese enters this body, many things in Vehicle's body change: the hormones, secretions from the pituitary glands, the thyroid, pancreas, blood circulation, the heart…all these are Old Chinese's, and these take their toll on the Vehicle. We are now going to conduct what Old Chinese calls 'Rejuvenation Circles. None of you have experienced anything of this sort, and it requires getting your hands and dirt under your fingernails in your garden, not by sitting back and listening to Old Chinese and you going away feeling wiser. When Old Chinese leaves you, he does not feel wise. Your wisdom will come from your inner understanding, and we are involved in that area.

If you listen to something in a church, temple or other institution, you listen to whomever talks to you and you leave saying, "Wasn't that beautiful." This is what your words convey, yet your aura is orange! If there is anything that Old Chinese cannot stand, it is a beautiful orange aura. Old Chinese appreciates ugly orange auras, but not beautiful ones! That will never happen again, for there needs to be individual participation in the spiritual growth beyond your subconscious. Your subconscious has never existed before this incarnation, and it will never exist again. Spiritual growth cannot come from the subconscious unless it has been acquired in your current lifetime. What you read in your subconscious is what you have put there, but if you close it, discard it, let a herd of wild buffalo run over it, then you will open up to your Higher Self. This is your goal.

You should also work on spiritual femininity. In this pre-cataclysmic period on your world, there are more females than at any other time. Not necessarily negative-polarity females, but more actual females. They have the ability, through their spiritual femininity to centre your internal world. A man cannot grow spiritually without that feminine influence. It is hard for some to accept, but it is true.

Then there are the children, travelling, moving and learning. We will establish and begin work on a completely new educational process for the world you live in. Because of your earthly laws, for the time being it must be called Religious Education, but even those words were orange! The Circle for Inner Truth is now a legally recognized entity on your world, a Church, of sorts. Through new developments in education for young ones that have not been seen since the time of Camelot and the lessons taught to Arthur by his teacher, Merlin.

Then, there is balance, helping your body to be balanced, not through strenuous exercise in a big building that builds your muscles, only to turn to fat three years later, but through learning easy and flowing movements. We will investigate health and nutrition, and ways to cope as your world becomes less able to feed its population.

While Old Chinese is in full trance, he will be beside Vehicle to provide counsel for inner growth, no more, no less. Each of you can grow beyond Old Chinese, and it is Old Chinese's hope that before the Vehicle's soul departs his body, that each of you will have moved beyond our teachings, reaching your Higher Self, and communicating with the world in all its and your beautiful vibrations.

When you leave here, as summer approaches, consider the future. Those who have searched and found peace within themselves, created by their inner garden, will never be without food, money or shelter. Children grow, and so will you.

Consider what Old Chinese has said, and which path you are willing to follow – your own inner path is the most valuable. Of the seven levels of spirit communication, Old Chinese speaks to you from the sixth level. The seventh is your Higher Self, and this is what you will cultivate as time goes on. You say, "So much to say, so much to do." But your mind is like the tiger going after a deer, so consider these things regarding finding your Higher Self:

First – You have the ability to create your own inner garden within, wherever you are and you will no longer need a community or an institute.

Secondly – As you create this, you will be free from famine, disease and war.

Thirdly – It allows you to get to the point of evolution off this earthly plane.

Lastly – If Old Chinese ever says that what he said was The Way, The Word, or The Path, he would be withdrawn by his Masters, for they would not allow this to be said. The Vehicle will not allow this either, for if that happens, Old Chinese is withdrawn. Old Chinese will be the Vehicle for as long as he lives, subtle but strong, because we must protect your ability to develop your Higher Self, but without any form of external worship. Those who undergo Rejuvenation will become new entities, evolving and entering the Circle of the Rainbow and the Circle of the Orchard.

The Masters knew that you cannot teach inner peace through an institute or an organization. As the Masters died, their followers claimed that it was possible, saying,

"It is only in this temple that you will grow," instead of the physical temple you walk in each day.

Until you can build a community within yourself, a place to grow and work peacefully from, then no external community can stand, it would crumble and burn like the school of Pythagoras.

Finally each step that we teach is dedicated to the fertilisation of your inner garden. Know that as we give, love comes in return. This is true peace and beauty.

Because there are so many, Old Chinese will take six questions this evening – not sixty-six!

Q: Chung Fu, what's the difference between sitting down, meditating and hearing information about certain things, and just knowing or feeling it?

OC: There is no difference, just the degree or communicated aspect of the individual. Some will hear, some will see – it comes in different ways, in different patterns. Some of you may see it daily. Some of you bury it, or throw it in the garbage, and most of you do not even know it is there. You see it and you think, "What is that?"

It is there, you have the knowledge, which is what we build within your garden. Peace.

So many tips of tongues. For those that ask the question, consider the emperor and the gardener sitting within the garden, watching as things flow, work and then consider. As time moves on, one day it will be Old Chinese asking *you* the questions.

Q: Chung Fu, when you spoke of the subconscious you said in order to reach your Higher Self you have to discard it and have a herd of buffalo ride over it.

OC: Maybe two.

Q: Give or take a few.

OC: Two herds, not two water buffalo!

Q: You're so sharp, all the time!

OC: Old Chinese will answer you. You do not nail the door shut very tight. Let us say that you are walking down the street and you see someone and say, "That is the ugliest person I have ever seen." The reason you say that is because you have met them before in this life. By decreasing those thoughts, by affirming, "They are beautiful," the next time you see them, your first thought will be, "They are beautiful," before the negative thought arises. Your subconscious is like a book – if you replace the negative with a positive, when you reach that point again the positive thought will present itself before the negative one. That is what we mean by closing the door. It comes down to fear.

Fear is having noise within yourself, facing something that has caused you difficulty in the past. If you are walking along a precipice and you feel fear, say that you are a bird, that you have strength. Replace the thought that was formed perhaps thirty or forty years before, with a positive one. Soon all negativity will be replaced. The subconscious is the storehouse of the negative, not positive. Peace.

Q: Chung Fu, isn't putting replacement positive thoughts in the subconscious the same as positivity coming from the subconscious?

OC: In one sense, true, but the negative is the door, with you and your Higher Self being the light at the end of the tunnel. You are at one end and your subconscious is in the middle. Every time a negative thought comes the door of the subconscious opens and you cannot see the lights at the end of the tunnel. Replace it with a positive thought and it shuts, and you can see the light. Soon you will find that you will overcome the subconscious, for if you are doing good work or positive things, they are not recorded. You do not want them recorded. If you do something solely because you want your good deed recorded, this is not good. All the things that you do from your Higher Self do not record on your subconscious. The Nazarene eliminated the subconscious in the last three years of his life, nothing was recorded. Each of you have that ability. The communication, the peace and the positivity that comes forth from the Higher Self will not be recorded. Why do you have to record the good things you do?

Q: Isn't the reason attachment?

OC: Attachment to what?

Q: Well, what I was saying is that the snag in positive reinforcement is feeling, "My goodness, aren't I a great person..."

OC: What is a snag?

Q: A hook, catch, or problem...

OC: Peace. Snag is many things.

Q: When you were talking about thoughts that evolved, in terms of competition and emotions that fell like snow. Feelings of, "My goodness, aren't I developing, aren't I becoming spiritually elevate", isn't that attachment?

OC: Who is making that decision?

Q: It's a question, not a decision.

OC: Who is making that judgement that you are becoming spiritually elevated?

Q: Myself, my subconscious…

OC: You mean your subconscious says to you that you are becoming spiritually elevated?

Q: I say to myself, "My goodness, aren't I doing well," And feel, you know, inflated…

OC: That is good, no one should judge that, including yourself.

Q: Yeah, well, that's the trouble.

OC: There is no trouble in your world. You cannot show me one thing that is trouble.

Q: I guess I can't show you, it just feels that way sometimes.

OC: Feeling is a different thing. Consider the word that you use. Mistake, trouble, fault, guilt, all of these created to make you feel low. The Living Spirit does not recognise negativity, famine, poverty and does not recognise what you call Satan, which is your own creation so you have a place to unload all the bad things that you do not wish to be burdened with. The God Force does not recognise any of these things because to do so would mean becoming them. The only way you will understand these things is through the communication of a spirit Guide or a master. So, when you say there is trouble, it is a physical creation, not a spiritual one. When someone says you make a mistake you think, "Oh", but if someone told you that you had had an experience, you change. Words cause more problems of emotion than the actual emotion causes.

You are all beautiful, with different inflections and different feelings. If you say, "You are beautiful" to a female and you say it in red, you might find her in your physical arms, but not held close to your spiritual self. This is what we are talking of: coming to terms with words created by psychologists and theologians that you struggle with. It is not as hard as it seems. Most of you look into your subconscious and see turbulent waters. The ideal is to calm them so that your subconscious can mirror your Higher Self, not replace it. It is a reflection like the sun and the moon together. Peace.

Q: If you find yourself feeling resentment and anger towards another person, but you realise that the core of the problem is inside yourself, should you express this to the other person, or do the words make it worse. Is it better kept within you?

OC: It depends on what the other person has in their hands when you tell them, and it depends on where you are. If you feel anger toward another person, it is usually because of a weakness within yourself, not within the other person. If someone says to you, "The wart on the end of your nose is ugly," and you say, "I have no wart on the end of my nose, that makes me angry," that is their reality, why get upset about it? If they see warts on the end of your nose, that's their problem, not yours.

Understand that someone else's reality is just as important as yours. If they say, "Face reality," what they are actually saying is face *their* reality, not yours. Anger and resentment come from within because you realise that what has been said is either true or does not contain any truth at all. If it is not true, why get angry? The only reason you would get angry if it had no truth is because you have probably thought, "What if I *do* have a wart on the end of my nose?" Peace.

Q: Chung Fu, if you are in an environment where other people try to put their realities on you, and you are aware that it is you yourself who is causing…

OC: Old Chinese will answer your thoughts, not your words. When you are in somebody else's environment and your own inner environment causes difficulties, who has the difficulties, them or you? Who judges the difficulty? They may say because you say this or that, or behave in a particular way, or have a particular aura, which is their reality, but what of yours? If you cannot get along with someone else's reality, then you must go by another path, for if you are on someone else's reality path, you might have to endure brambles, while your own path is strewn with roses.

Remember that Lao-Tzu, Confucius, Buddha and the Nazarene all said, in one way or another, "Love your God, then love your neighbour as yourself." When you think of this remember firstly that the Living Spirit is within you. By loving yourself, you automatically love the God Force. If you love yourself, you automatically love your neighbour for they have the same Living Spirit inside them that you have within yourself. But for some reason, it becomes so confused and difficult in a religious framework that says you must love everything else in the same way as others do. If you love the God Force within you, you love the God Force in everyone else. That does not mean you have to love the personality of the individual or that you even have to endure their company. When you cannot bear to be around someone, that usually indicates they are not expressing their latent God Force through their personality. Should this happen, go within yourself, and love yourself, which in turn means loving the God Force. Besides, anyone who does not express their God Force is boring, and lacks creativity. Each of us expresses our own God Force. Love yourself and rebuild your garden.

~ ~ ~ ~ ~ ~ ~ ~ ~

In Old China a sage sat under a plum tree. His student asked him, "Teacher, what is life?" The teacher said, "Look around you, what do you see?" The student replied, "I see the Livingness of birds, of insects and the trees. I see the Livingness of the animals and the morning dew." The teacher then asked, "And what else do you see?" The student answered, "I see the beauty of the stars, and smell the fragrance of flowers." The teacher said, "But you still have not seen life, for life is within those things, but what you see is only physical." The student said, "But how do I see within, how do I eliminate the senses so I can see within?" And the teacher said, "You see within by knowing that you are the Living Spirit, and you were created with an internal sense. You see the God Force in the plum tree and the teacher." With that, the student went away, confused and unsure what to do. The teacher bowed his head and went within to communicate with the student who had walked away.

Blessings and Peace to you all.

~ I am free from all bondage and limitation. I am, free indeed ~

RESPECT FOR ALL LIVING THINGS

London – 18 February 1975

Blessings and Peace to you all and may the Living Spirit that is all life forms come forward and give you peace and protection within yourself. Blessings and Peace.

Tonight Old Chinese wants to talk to you about respecting all living things and spiritual nutrition. First you must understand that you are students in the university of physical and material experience. What you learn during your many lifetimes is to step above the physical experience, which is your evolutionary goal. However, accompanying you on your path are different spiritual beings in many dimensions and different evolutionary areas. Not only do we have the elements – air, water, fire and earth – but we have the spirits that dwell in all living things who are also evolving. As you evolve, so too the highest elemental spirits evolve from earth to air to water, to sun or fire. Without these spirits nothing could live, breathe or procreate, and respect for all living things starts by respecting these elements. Respect what you do with fire and how you utilise it. Respect the water you drink, that purifies and nourishes the Earth, allowing billions of living creatures to live. Respect the air that carries pollen and seeds, that allows the birds to fly and you to breathe. Respect the earth you stand on.

By respecting the elements and all living things, Earth will maintain its balance and you will not have the great cataclysmic change. In respecting all living things, do not neglect air, water, earth and fire.

There are some evolutionary processes that you may not understand, such as those hidden deep within atoms and molecules. Some processes go even deeper than that, but we are addressing things you can see and are part of your physical plane.

There are four main categories, which then sub-divide into an upper and lower order: minerals, plants, animals and man. In each of these kingdoms there is a living, spiritually evolving entity, with either a group or individual spiritual identity. How you view and respect these things is also part of your own spiritual evolution. In the mineral kingdom you have the lower minerals: rock and sand, right beneath your feet and alive, but only at the very earliest beginnings of their evolution. Man's use of them will help them evolve. In the mineral kingdom you also have the higher order: jewels and gemstones, which have experienced many evolutions to reach that stage. There are the four key jewels: ruby which embodies fire, amethyst for water, crystal for the air and black jade for earth. There are many others of course, but these are the higher spiritual elements of the mineral kingdom, and when they are acknowledged, respected and valued they will grow. Over millions of years, some spirits will dedicate their existence to the earth aspect and will eventually become a gem, enjoyed and creatively used by Man. Even if Man breaks up that gem into smaller pieces, that spirit will evolve by such recognition and use.

Secondly, the plant kingdom, wherein the lower plants are root plants or root vegetables, and the higher order are the fruiting plants. The evolutionary spirits within root plants are not very advanced, being merely in the early stage of their evolution. No root vegetable contains more vitamins and minerals than those contained in the higher vegetable and fruiting plant order. You should remember that higher spiritual elements are found in fruit plants and vegetables. You must understand that taking the fruit from a tree, a berry from the bush, or a melon from the vine does not kill the whole plant and its Livingness remains.

By respecting all living things you show respect to spiritual evolution and this should be observed not only in Mankind, but also in the plant and animal kingdoms. By concentrating your efforts and appreciative thoughts toward fruiting plants, you are helping their spirit evolve. It is common for root vegetables to be mass produced and harvested in such a way that their spirit is cut short and, in large fields where this type of picking happens, there are group spirits. You should be aware also that these are more exposed to chemical fertilizers and pollution of the earth than other plants and vegetables. It is hard to help such spirits evolve by acknowledging them unless they are in your own garden or on land dedicated to this type of spiritually aware agriculture. In making your decision on which fruit or plant to eat you are honouring and aiding the evolution of higher level spirit. When you select a fruit, you do so knowing that the tree is still living and that it has given you its fruit, for the tree is evolving to a higher being also. But when you select a lettuce or a cabbage, you know it was once part of a group spirit, with little Life Force within it, and less vitamin and mineral content than your body needs. The fact that you eat lettuce or cabbage is not going to make you a higher or lower being, but it is going to make you conscious of honouring spiritual evolution, whereby you accept that spirits are giving fruit to you, in the same way that Mankind produces fruit in the form or word, action and creativity. Therefore, those who eat these vegetables are not to be looked down on, and those of you who are working toward a higher spiritual evolution, should concentrate on minerals, plants, animals and people that possess the highest spiritual levels. If you wish to grow spiritually do not ask someone who is in their first life on the earth plane, who might sometimes be a severely disabled child or someone from a spiritually barren society. You should seek out those who are in tune with all evolution.

Amongst animals, the lower order contains insects, fish and reptiles that possess a group spirituality. The higher ones are those with legs such as cats, dogs, horses, cows and water mammals, such as the porpoise, for these respond to the love of Man. Although they begin with a group spirit, they can develop more individualised spirits when they interact with Man, and spirits enter these animals' bodies so they can be loved by Man. With reptiles, you are not dealing with a separate spirit, they also have a group soul. You have an individual spirit whereas a reptile or an insect has a group spirit driving it, overseen by a Guide. And so, you take the fruits of the higher animals: milk from cows, eggs from poultry, or the honey from bees. What about the eggs from a fish? That would still be of the lower spiritual order. No matter whether it is fish, snake, spider or bug, none of them have the same protein, vitamin, mineral value, gram for gram, as the fruits of the cow, sheep, goat or bird. When you look at these four kingdoms you will see that it is the fruits of these that have the highest spiritually evolved state. *You are trying to produce your own fruit by acknowledging that you are not your brother's keeper, that you are your own keeper first, and you will pull toward you people whom you can teach, learn from and be in tune with.*

Those who honour the fruits of each kingdom will, in turn, be honoured by each of those kingdoms. The results of this are beyond even your wildest imagination – not being suffocated by sand or dirt, for the elemental spirits reside within those and they would not allow it. You will not die under a falling tree or eating a poisonous plant, nor by tooth or claw of an animal, but by a natural death and having made evolutionary progress.

In old China, a gardener went to the four corners of his garden dedicating it to the spirits, waiting for the spiritual evolution of his plants, minerals and animals therein. Whether radish, beet or fruit from the trees, the spirits in that garden were evolving. But in an animal context, it did not mean killing an animal, for animals only evolve as you love and give it care, not if you kill them.

At no time since your last cataclysm has any great sage or teacher ever said, "It is time for this animal or that plant to die - take its life." No one has that authority and not even the Living Spirit will do it, and so you cannot either. But as you evolve, your awareness will develop and you will see the fragility of these spirits. No great sage or teacher in any cataclysm has advocated taking the life of an animal or plant, so the key to knowing your world is understanding the four elements, for they are a spiritual evolution of the angelic force, and they work with the spirits that work with you. Understand that if you want to evolve to the highest spiritual evolution concentrate in the higher areas of each of the four kingdoms. You should never kill an animal.

Now, what of the trees, that are cut and used for lumber and paper? You should not judge those who do this for that is their state of evolution, but if you respect all living things, you will not do it yourself. A tree is of high spiritual evolution, but its fruit is often ignored, its wood more sought after to be cut down than to be honoured, like your saints and sages that are cut down, only later to be honoured and their absence mourned. That is a great sadness, but it is the truth. Paper has created much education and understanding. Lumber has given you warmth and shelter, but it has been abused. You do not need as many books as you have, and you do not need as much wood as you burn and build with, yet you are not held responsible.

If you are in spiritual free-flow, alert to your Higher Self, you will use the wood of trees that have died and are strong, avoiding dead wood from trees that are weak, filled with bacteria and insects. The fact that you are involved in construction or other uses of wood is a different state of consciousness and spiritual evolution. Using paper as a means to spiritual growth and enlightenment is both wise and justified, but if it is used to the detriment of Mankind, then you are using it wrongly.

Minerals seem to last the longest in your world, and need the longest time to evolve, whether it is brick or stone. The Great Pyramid had quarries dedicated to it before construction began, and it is in stone and minerals that spirits remain longest. In the compression of mud and brick one finds a concentrated group consciousness. As you view the destruction of trees from a spiritual standpoint, so too should you honour minerals by not destroying them.

All living things contain the capacity to elevate you above this earthly plane. There is life in bacteria and the amoeba. If a plant becomes diseased, you should love it and give it care. If it was out in the wilds, it is responsible for its own evolution, but once Man takes responsibility for a tree or a plant he is duty-bound to tend to it and show kindness to that life. Whilst caring for that plant, any negative thought on your part will be picked up and that plant will die. The higher you evolve, the more beautiful you and your plant will become.

Respect trees and plants, giving them the honour they deserves and they will serve you, ultimately giving you the peace you seek. There will be a time in your world when paper will never be used again and you will not need it because you will have the ability to tap into any consciousness, past, present and even future.

Respecting all living things is key in your search and attainment of free-flowing spiritual energy. There are many avenues and methods that you can take in this search. By respecting all living things you create a protective aura around you that will shield you from each of the different kingdoms. By developing higher spiritual understanding of living things, you will step out of a hostile world.

The elements of fire, water, air and earth that control Man, animal, plant and mineral, combined with your respect for all living things, will allow you to reincarnate off the earthly plane.

The pollution of air, water and the earth is not caused by burning the plant kingdom, nor does the animal kingdom cause pollution. Fire in the mineral kingdom sometimes ravages in order to cleanse. Keep warm using what is around you, but more importantly using the warmth of your consciousness.

Finally, what of the leather shoes or belt that you wear, or other animal products you use? Animals die, this is inevitable, and the use of their hides is acceptable, for they have left you that gift. However, to take the life of an animal purely to obtain leather is a different thing. Thousands of years ago, there were people who could prepare an animal's spirit before death, but there have been none capable of this for more than 2,000 years. In those times, the killing of animals was for the growth of Man and spiritual evolution. At that time, those on a lower evolutionary level ate only roots and plants, and did not partake of meat. You, however, are more evolved than this, no longer reliant on the flesh of animals.

You must respect all living things, but you must respect yourself the most, both spiritually and nutritionally. You embody the Living Spirit and nothing is higher or lower than you. By loving yourself and expressing the Living Spirit you are respecting living things. Sages, saints and masters come to give you direction, to turn the light on in a darkened room, but nothing in this world controls you.

The sage or master is there merely to lead you to the light switch. Anyone who says that you are not in control is misleading you. You are the highest evolution and expression of the Living Spirit in a physical world whose shackles often prevent you connecting to your Higher Self. By loving yourself, Mankind and your inner self, you are respecting the Living Spirit. You may be friendly with the exterior self, but it is the interior realm that should be loved.

Your body is not designed to consume everything in your world – your digestive system is not intended to eat meat. Your stomach, large and small intestine, your second stomach, the duodenum, and colon are not intended to digest meat. You are herbivorous, and the meat you ingest comes from herbivorous animals. The protein of milk products, eggs, soya, rice, grains and vegetables is the purest kind of protein, vitamin and mineral. Honour your body, your vehicle for the physical world.

Do not combine fruits or melons, eat them separately. Do not combine carbohydrates with proteins, nor fats or sugars with protein. Combine carbohydrates with vegetables, protein and vegetables, sweets and fats with vegetables.

There are carbohydrates that share some characteristics of proteins and vice versa. That which has the most carbohydrate is a carbohydrate, and that which contains the most protein is indeed a protein.

There are three food groups you must be cautious of: refined sugars, salt and wheat products that lack the wheat husk, or wheat germ. Focus instead on key nutritional foods: molasses, yeast, yoghurt, citrus juices, wheat-germ, and of course, the plants and vegetables that produce fruit that do not require the killing of the entire plant. These are the main things to consider in your spiritual nutrition, honouring your body and yourself.

So, by respecting yourself and all living things you will evolve to newer evolutions, the work of your masters and Guides having been accomplished, which in turn allows them to evolve further. You will be able to feel, see, hear and touch the beauty of all kingdoms inside yourself and beyond.

~ ~ ~ ~ ~ ~ ~ ~ ~ ~

In Old China, a sage sat under a tree that was laden with delicious plums, with two students sitting nearby. One student asked him, "What should we do in life?" The sage replied, "Respect yourself, respect the plum tree, and by respecting these two things, your life will be fulfilled." "But what about you, Teacher?" said the students, "Should we not respect you?" And the teacher said, "If you respect yourself and you respect those things that give you nutrition for yourself, you respect all living things."

We have talked before of spiritual evolution, how each and every living things has the Living Spirit within it. Yours is the physical universe, as you stand upon your Earth and look up at a star, you see the light, beauty and clarity. All that you see is a creation of the physical plane that your men of science urge you to see, but millions of other dimensions exist that you do not yet see because they possess different vibrations and evolutions. The spirit world where Old Chinese teaches from is always the centre line, where the vibrations are stable and consistent. After the reincarnation cycle he always returns to the spirit world.

The Living Spirit which is within every living thing is the Life Force, the soul, and yours is not the only one, but it is unique. Remember that the mineral, plant and animal kingdoms possess group souls. A mineral, stone or rock has a group spirit that it reincarnates into and stays there for a long as its spiritual evolution requires. It will evolve slowly, over many centuries, perhaps a stone within a mountain that Man may never see, but it is there. The only way they can evolve is by Man noticing and appreciating them. When a man picks up a piece of jade and begins to identify with it, the group within that piece of jade severs itself from the group and becomes an individual soul for as long as that man loves it. If that person throws it away, that individual soul will go back to the group, but if man keeps it, it will evolve into higher dimensions and other worlds. As is evolves, another part of the jade group will reincarnate. A person who has jade or crystal could be responsible for the evolution of perhaps fifty or sixty different souls. It is through the love of man that the mineral spirit can evolve to other worlds.

In the plant kingdom, the same principle applies. If a person loves a plant, respects and nurtures it, the group spirit will break off and leave a part there which evolve. It is a higher evolution so needs more identification, and so by picking the fruit the tree's spirit can evolve. If you have a tree that you have loved, causing it to become an individual soul, but you then cut it down the individual soul will return to the group and you will have hindered its evolution. Whenever you pick a fruit from a plant or tree the spirit within rejoices because your identification of its soul makes it live on. The root vegetables are of a lower order and if you pull one up after loving and nurturing it, its spirit will return to the group soul, but you can take the carrot or cabbage, just trimming the tops, pull back the leaves and help their evolution, but this is rarely done. If you have grass growing in a field but you wish to plant something, wait for the grass to turn brown or has died away naturally before you turn it into the ground because then there is no individual soul within it.

If you care for an animal, the animals are pulled to man for love. There is no Karma in the animal kingdom, those that kill one another do so for genetic and hormonal reasons, not because of Karma. Lions and tigers are group souls and only become individual souls when Man loves them and helps them to develop individual souls. An animal kept in the wild will retain its group soul. Your anthropologists and zoologists prefer that you return them to the wild. It may be good for the instinct of the animal, but it does not help the evolution of their soul. It is a great responsibility, like a Down Syndrome child who relies on you and your love in their first reincarnation of a new spirit. Having never been on your earthly plane before their soul needs all your love. If they are not loved or wanted, and are put into an institution where they do not receive love, their soul probably will not reincarnate again on your physical plane.

Loving and milking a cow evolves its individual spirit, breaking it off from the group soul. If you kill the cow after giving it love, you are not helping it progress or respecting the concept of respect for all living things. Eating meat or fish is not allowing the individual soul to evolve. If you wear leather belts or shoes you are wearing products that you need not kill to obtain, but by wearing leather you cannot say that you are prolonging the force of the animal.

You do not feel you should kill your fellow man, nor that your fellow man should have a price placed on his head, and if a man dies through you your actions then you are responsible. Trees die to make the books that you read.

The Karmic effect of causing an individual soul to return to a group spirit is worse than the actual action of killing it. Those who cut down a fruit tree have a greater Karmic effect than those who cut down thousands of pine trees that have a group soul within them. Domesticated animals like the pig, sheep or goat that are used by man have individual soul, and you should prolong their life allowing them to be of service for the milk or eggs they provide. If a cow dies naturally its skin can be used for the leather and you are not involved in its death. You are only part of the cow's death if you chose to eat its meat. Your consciousness should be saying, "I am not eating anything that has been killed. I am nourishing my body by helping the evolution of other spirits."

Spirits of water are destroyed by being pulled into your sanitation systems, or in the air that you breathe or blow pollution into from industrial furnaces and cars. Man is the only entity born with an individual soul and it is his responsibility to help other group souls. Man should respect himself and understand that he was not designed to eat meat, being created with a short intestine, and he was intended to be a fruit gatherer. Your bodies cannot take meat, they are not intended for this, and they never will. The native American Indians were able to kill an animal, but also able to release their group soul, not the individual soul. A thousand years ago those Indians did not eat meat but when they started to eat meat they created Karma. The spirits in water will not react to the Indian or to those who have taken the life form that they are responsible for. Man has always had trouble interacting with the four elements, for if a man is at peace with himself he will never have trouble with fire. Similarly, if he is at peace with animals he will always be in control of water. If he is at peace with the plant kingdom, the wind and air will serve him. If he is at peace with minerals and gems, the earth will serve and provide for him.

Within all animals, plants and minerals there are spirits, some call them sylphs, gnomes or fairies, and these are individual evolutionary patterns that are evolving in a completely different way. Try to see the evolution in flowers and plants. By pruning a flower or a tree you are not killing it, rather you are helping it to grow, like cutting your fingernails or hair.

The evolution of your individual soul is of paramount importance. Without this you are not in tune with the world, you are only in tune with the material and physical and you are not respecting yourself. Respect all living things, for as the spirits evolve through your love, so do you also evolve. Only by loving these kingdoms will it come together and you will reincarnate out. You are responsible for yourself and all that is around you.

Blessings and peace, and may the Living Spirit give you the energy you seek.

~ I meet all situations with full realisation of the power of Spirit to guide, guard and sustain me ~

THE CATACLYSM

London – 28 November 1974

Blessings and Peace to you all and may the light that comes forth in all things unfold within the Livingness of your life. For it is in this Livingness that you understand your destiny. Peace.

The Living Spirit is in all things, far beyond your imagination and intellectual perceptions. Everything that you see and breathe, everything that you are, everything that you were, and everything that you walk on or gather around you contains the Living Spirit. Cosmic Energy, the Universal Mind, the God Force, or the Living Spirit are all one and the same. It is not something that you can visualise or categorise, nor can it be described easily in a book. It is an energy, a vibration, a Livingness that never dies. It is incomprehensible to the mind of Man, who tries continually to make the Living Spirit comprehensible; a futile endeavour, destined for frustration. As you look up into the night, you see stars, universes and galaxies, billions of light years away. Each one of these is a living entity, each of them an energy source that has sent forth light, and their vibrations are an energy, impossible to put one's fingers on.

However, on your world, because the Living Spirit is in the floor, sky, trees, animal and within yourself, certain natural patterns evolve. Your skin and blood contains the Living Spirit, and is a perfect combination. The Living Spirit is also in the instinctual aspect of an animal and in the petals of a flower whose colour and scent are combined to show the perfection of its living essence. On Earth, in the process of fertilisation, in the decaying bodies of insects, trees and plants, the Living Spirit is constantly regenerating. But certain aspects of the Living Spirit do not meld or come together. Even though they are the Living Spirit, they do not mesh – the pieces do not fit together. Your world is arranged in a naturally ordered aspect, rock upon rock, of perfect design and in order, so when things are not put together correctly, they do not bond, or come together. They reject, as do the poles, in opposition of each other. And that is what has happened in your world many times.

Approximately 7,000 years ago, the Earth had more inhabitants than it has now. Civilisations were scattered throughout the world in dwellings that are no longer visible. There were rivers, lakes and orchards that are not in the places they are now. These civilisations revered the material aspect and liked the generation of electricity, the generation of mobility, of the movement of things. They reaped gas, oil, and coal from the earth; resources that allowed them to be warm and move swiftly through the air, but gradually created a pollutant aspect. Even though the pollution also possessed Livingness, there was a rejection, not a melding.

You can feel this rejection. When you walk on the heights of a mountain, feeling the freshness of the air, you feel at one with Nature. But walk through a city on a smog filled morning, you will find it hard to breathe and want to escape. The spiritual vibrations that make up the Livingness of both air and pollutant reject each other and they must move to different places. The purer element moves away allowing the pollutant to take over.

7,000 years ago there were predictions that the Earth could not survive because coal and gas were in dwindling supply, and the fish from the sea were dying in polluted waters. There was not enough air to allow Man to live with an ever increasing population. However, people who were in tune with the spirit of Livingness gradually gravitated toward each other, not following a particular God Force, religion or creed, but instead by withdrawing to themselves. They came to understand that by being in tune with Nature, their environment and the elements – fire, earth, water and air, they became part of a vibration that had linked civilisations throughout the cataclysmic periods of the Earth.

And so, the water, air, and Earth were polluted and the God Forces could not meld and blend together. There was a massive rejection, just as you have rejection between opposing magnetic forces, which created a vibration so immense it caused the North and South poles to switch places in a matter of seconds. Ocean waves over three miles high circled the globe in the vibrational change, while areas of land rose and other parts were driven under as the Earth split apart. Great movements of water pushed civilisations aside and churned them under as a plough tills the soil. For fifteen to twenty minutes, the Earth was encircled by an unbelievable force and power. However, small pockets of civilisation survived. These survivors, in tune with themselves, not blindly following gods or philosophies or faith, realised that by being in tune with the Nature and by projecting Livingness, or the correct spiritual attitude toward life, they would always be in the right place at the right time.

In the parts of your world now known as China, South America, Central America, the Great Plains, Egypt, Nepal, Greece and Scandinavia, billions were killed in an instant, but twenty or thirty thousand people survived. In a matter of moments, the Earth had restored its natural balance and things began once again. Each of these civilisations understood Livingness and with the projection of their minds created new temples and pyramids. They understood the vibration of the Sun and were able to travel great distances by projecting the mind into the body, not needing coal and ore from the Earth. With their ability to communicate with the spirits inside a plant, the sylphs of the air, the undines of the water, with the salamanders of the fire, and with the gnomes of the Earth, they bridged dimensions by disciplining the body and letting the spiritual aspect beyond the mind unfold.

From simple mountain caves they began to create civilisations again. The first generation had a solid understanding of the cataclysm and the chaos that came from it. Unlike your times now, when there is a great spiritual darkness, theirs was a time of spiritual enlightenment and the Earth underwent a complete rejuvenation through spiritual understanding of Nature and their surroundings. They rebuilt the vibration by understanding the Livingness of things and they taught their children how to do so. Many children who had survived the cataclysm understood vibration and energy, but their children's children began to say, "Cataclysm? You must be out of your mind, like a buffalo stung by a bee. Worlds turning and civilisations falling, that is impossible. Things are so peaceful, why should I stay here? Why should I concern myself with the disciplines of body and mind, when there is a world that I want to see, and great oceans I want to cross?"

And so, one by one, from all parts of the world their children departed, searching, seeking and the world began to develop. Ancient wisdom, perfectly manifested in the I-Ching from China, the mysteries of the Olympiad and the Delphic oracle in Greece, the Great Pyramid, the Incans,

Mayans, and the Indians of the Great Plains, were slowly lost. The abilities of transference and travelling great distances in minutes, disappeared as knowledge of the ancients died, hidden within the walls and the vaults of the pyramids. Their wisdom was lost until Masters such as Lao Tzu, Buddha, Confucius, Zoroaster, the Nazarene and Pythagoras appeared. They restored this knowledge, tying a knot in the threads of wisdom that had previously unravelled. These Masters said that you did not have to be in the shade of an inner temple, that you could live again by understanding of the Livingness of things, and that the God Force was internal, not external.

The Earth's resources were depleted and the water polluted. It has taken more than 6,000 years for the coal to return to the Earth, because of the time and great geological pressures needed to create gas and gems. For 6,000 years, Man had lived without these things, yet in a period as short as most of your lives, Man had destroyed all they had built in that time. But it is a cycle, and has happened time and time again, a part of the evolution of learning to deal with the physical plane.

By relaxing their whole body, they were able to move from one place to another in an instant – not by astral projection, but by an actual physical transportation. They walked upon water, handled fire, and worked harmoniously with the earth, by honouring all living things. When you can feel and understand the heartbeat of these ancient wisdoms, you will be in tune with what is going on in your world. There are people who honour these elements, using them for spiritual growth of the highest order, but the masses are more concerned about material belongings, not in understanding the God Force within themselves. Now, 300 generations removed from the last cataclysm, the challenge to overcome the physical world is still being faced. The physical does not matter.

In the not too distant future, the poles will switch again, resulting in a renewal of the Earth, and those who are spiritually in tune will survive. It will take almost 1,000 years before there is a re-circulation of any type of spiritual beings, for in the beginning there, will be only those who are spiritually attuned. Then, as the population grows, those who need to learn more will return and will also have a period in the spirit world to understand their evolution.

But what of now? You are still caught within the great cycle, not remembering your past, sometimes not fathoming what Old Chinese has said about the Cataclysm, unable to comprehend that in a twinkling of an eye, great canyons could be created or destroyed, and whole civilisations destroyed by monumental winds and waters churning around the Earth's surface, only to be dug up 6,000 years later by scientists searching for oil and coal.

Your life is a cycle, like the seasons of your Earth, and is the university of physical experience. You were reincarnated into your parentage to experience and learn from what you are now involved in, and should feel no guilt with regard to what you have or have not learned, because what you are is precisely what you should be, which is the best projection for this time and this age. You are at the threshold of spiritual understanding, where everything that has been placed in your subconscious through your five senses can be discarded. You can step beyond it and close the door by realising that you are the God Force, projecting the energy and positivity that is within you now. You are in control and should know that you are eternal, immortal and universal.

And so, nothing you have done is wrong. There is no sin. How can there be sin when you are the God Force within? The sin would be *not* recognising that you are the God Force and projecting it through your personality. But that is not really sin, it is merely ignorance. No matter what you were as a child or what your married life is like now, you should start to see yourself as the God Force within. You will say, "Old Chinese, your words sound so easy, but to practice them is like trying to peel the skin off a live water buffalo". This is because faith has become a thing either in or out of reach and the belief that you cannot change anything. To honour nature and the Livingness of things, you must also honour your body, through individual discipline and be in control of your life. Freedom is bondage, and discipline is freedom.

If you allow a small child total freedom at school you will find that as the child grows he cannot choose for himself. Man, in essence, is a disciplined being. It is through discipline that he steps beyond the physical and material, not through freedom. Not through sexual use and misuse, not through flaunting what Man has created, but by realising that discipline allows the spirit to step beyond the physical. The spirit cannot step beyond something that it experiences everything within your world. But that does not mean that sexual relations are wrong. They are very right if they are for individual growth and you feel afterward that you have been uplifted.

You are a projection of the God Force, projecting differently from the Vehicle or Quinta Joy, a different entity to the person next to you. Know that your projection is unique, creative and important. An insect projects the Living Spirit differently to the rose, just as you project differently from the person across the street. Your world often gets caught up in the idea of "sameness" – that you must project like this person or that religion, but who wants robots? The robots of Atlantis died in the last cataclysm, but there are those who say that they were also under the guidance of unknown forces and that some of them survived.

What you are is what you should be, trying to find an inner peace through tuning your body in so that you control it and it does not control you. Do not let society tell you what to do, when to do it, and how to do it. You have no freedoms. If you live within the legal boundaries of society, there is nothing that you really own. Try not paying your government what you owe them on your property and see how long you own it. Try not paying your taxes and see the freedom that you have. You think you live in freedom? No, not within your governmental systems, only within yourself because there no country in your world that is free. True freedom can only be felt when your society does not control you, when you step above it and you do not worry about the way it projects itself.

Do not worry that you could become poor as the monetary system in your world collapses, because a bean is green instead of yellow. If your government says, "We no longer like green beans, only yellow beans" your country will no longer eat green beans. You, however, were born into a time, a nation, and a universe, to learn to step above such concerns, by living in free-flowing spirituality and knowing that you control your body, your financial system and that your world does not control you. The more things you have, the more you are controlled.

You are like the third generation after the last cataclysm. You say, "It cannot be, I only believe in what I see, feel and hear. Therefore, I am going out in search of answers" Instead of going outward, go within. Neither the Nazarene nor Buddha is your saviour because *you* are the God Force. Awaken yourself, for Old Chinese cannot do it, no religion in this world can do it, only you can. Everyone has this ability and if you project your positivity, and the beauty within, you will be at the right place at the right time.

So be it. You may ask your questions.

Q: In 1983, all the planets of this solar system will be aligned in a straight line. What effect will this have on the Earth?

OC: One moment please, while the Hermetic checks with a higher spiritual force. Next question, we will answer that when he returns in a moment.

Q: What force controls the cycles?

OC: The force is the evolution of the Living Spirit. It is like a puzzle. When you take a piece out of the puzzle, it becomes unbalanced. When you take three or four pieces out and you re-arrange them, it becomes misshapen and soon, in desperation, you will jumble it up. When pieces are removed and placed incorrectly with others, then this energy force is misused and it becomes unbalanced. Peace.

The answer in regards to the alignment of the Earth and the planets you have in mind: Hermetic tells Old Chinese that there have been great predictions of doom and destruction. If it is so, it will not be because of the aligning of these planets. There will be some tidal and seasonal changes, some extreme weather, but it will not cause great catastrophes. They are projecting wrongly – and besides, the planets' energies will be pulling off one another, not creating a combined energy force. Peace.

Q: Who or what was Krishna?

OC: This is an individual who lived in the previous cataclysm, a man that walked the Earth like Lao Tzu, Confucius and Buddha. He was a being like Zeus, or the god Wodan, who were actually men in other cataclysms. If you look beyond the Krishnivic tradition, you will see it is not a worship of a God, but of a power source. Because Man is what he is, he creates an individual to embody that power source. Peace.

Q: Does the Devil exist?

OC: Only in the minds of people. The God Force is positive thought, recognised through the Livingness of things. Think of what the Devil would be: always aligned to things that do not have Livingness within. The devil is a creation of Man because Man does not want to take the blame for the creation of cataclysms. In essence, the Devil is negative thought creating catastrophic elements and events within the physical world, causing man to say, "I could not create this." It is like a person who rises every day and says, "This is going to be a bad day." They walk out, are hit by a car and die. People say, "Life is against me, it must be the Devil or Satan" a concept that began by the simple thought many years ago: "This is a bad day." Peace.

Q: Why do spiritual travellers always mention light?

OC: Old Chinese's current existence is in another dimension, two dimensions beyond yours. Because his energy is so bright and so powerful, we must project the soul down through the last reincarnation of Old Chinese via the Vehicle. If Old Chinese entered this room as he appears in *his* dimension, the room would ignite into flames immediately. This is not because Old Chinese is a higher being, but because of his particular energy pattern. If you entered a dimension two below you, your vibration would cause great trauma and even death. Consider the ants that Man is constantly stepping on. It is a different vibration, a different energy. Peace.

Q: Do animals have spirits?

OC: There is a group soul in animals. Let us take for instance, the tiger. When a tiger is born, it is part of a group tiger soul. But if you take that tiger into your home and begin to love it, the tiger is severed from the group soul and it becomes individual through interaction with man. In that way there can be projection and evolution from your path. If the tiger is returned to the wild, the group soul returns. Animals evolve only through the love of Man. The animals whom Men love most are the dog and cat, hunters and meat eaters of your world that, with Man's love, can be taken beyond that particular stage of their evolution. Peace.

Q: Can you tell me more about the UFOs we hear so much about?

OC: Your initials do not match thought forms in the brain. What are you speaking of?

Q: We hear so much about these UFOs – Unidentified Flying Objects

OC: Old Chinese understands now. A three letter word, UFO, with your mental image does not tell Old Chinese what it is. What you call unidentified flying objects are not from other worlds in your universe but from other dimensions projecting into this one. Not necessarily higher dimensions, but in a different element of physical projection. They bridge these dimensions and it is not their intention to cause harm. They come through in freak changes, because there are places in your world where you can project from one dimension into another. Often it will be an accident, but there are, in essence, no accidents in your world. It depends on how highly attuned the individual going into these places is. These entities from other dimensions will sometimes travel from one dimension to another by being out of tune with their own particular environment. Peace.

Q: There is a current theory about the Earth being hollow. The author claims that other planets are also hollow and he gave reasons for this. Can you comment on this?

OC: Old Chinese cannot comment on the author or book but can tell you that you are not living on a hollow Earth, that it is very sound and that there is great energy within. It is as sound as your water is solid as liquid has mass. If you fall from 2,000 feet onto water or fall 2,000 feet onto earth, you have a better chance of surviving falling onto the earth than you do onto water. There is solid mass liquid within the Earth, it is not empty or hollow. But it is true that asteroids, other dimension moons and your moon have an element of hollowness within them. Peace.

Q: Why did you choose Marshall?

OC: Because he is weak, he is not a high being, it is in his evolutionary path to meet many people in your world, and because his Higher Self and Old Chinese agreed, before his reincarnation. He is just a vehicle, a channel for an energy force, for Old Chinese has a teacher and his teacher has a teacher, whose teacher has a teacher. We teach with the objective of letting you step above what is here. Peace.

~ ~ ~ ~ ~ ~ ~ ~ ~ ~

In Old China, a sage and a student walked along a path, and came upon a man sitting under a tree moving to and fro. The student turned and in a whisper told his teacher, "That is a crazy man, he is touched in his head. He has bees in his skull. He is as unpredictable as the rain and wind." The teacher walked up to the man and asked his student, "What is that man sitting under?" The student said, "It is a tree." The teacher asked the crazy man, "What is that you are sitting under?" The crazy man said, "It is a projection of the life force. It produces buds in the spring and shelter for the birds that come and make nests. It gives shade to the traveller and warmth in the winter to those who want to get out of the wind. Its leaves renew the ground beneath and it produces fruit in the fall." The teacher turned to the student and said, "What is that there?" The student said, "That is a stream." The teacher then asked the crazy man "What is that there?" The crazy man said, "That is the liquid of Life. It feeds the grass, the flowers the birds, the animals and men, whenever it flows. It goes to the ocean, returns to the air and it is replenished by the rain. It is Livingness." The teacher then turned to the student and said, "What is that there?" The student said, "That is a meadow." The teacher said to the crazy man, "What is that there?" The crazy man replied, "That is a field of grass and flowers, a field full of insect and animal life, where the butterfly and the bee are busy collecting pollen. Where the smells are many and it is filled with life and beauty." The teacher then turned to the student and said, "What is that there?" Seeing that he had been made to look a fool, the student replied, "That is the path away from here. It is the path goes to beautiful cities, to the great city of Li Po, to rivers that have many living things on it, to the castles of the emperor. That is that path." The teacher asked the crazy man, "What is that there?" And the madman replied, "It is a path away from the tree, the stream and the field."

May the Living Spirit in all life come forward and give you peace.

~ Only good can come to me because only good comes out of me ~

POSITIVITY

London – 5 December 1974

Blessings and Peace to you all. May the Living Spirit that lies deep within you come forward in a surge of beauty and give you the peace you seek incessantly from your life. Peace.

You are the Living Spirit within. You are the God Force within. The Living Spirit is not an external force that you must pray to seek outside of yourself. You do not have to seek favours from a loving God. The God Force in inside you, around you and in all living things - all vibrations, energy and in everything in this cosmos, all dimensions and all worlds, imagined or unimagined. You are in the Earth's cycle to learn, to step above the physical existence. Your body is a manifestation of the Living Spirit in its highest force on your physical plane, the way you express the soul you have created in this life. Through that Livingness is all power. Deep within you is the ability to connect with and summon an energy that has ten times the energy of your Sun, which is very similar in its essence.

The Sun is the Light that makes you live. The God Force is the Light that gives you life. The Sun warms you, as does the God Force. Do not think that you are merely a pawn in this world and begin to express yourself knowing that you are the God Force and how you express it brings great creativity. The same creativity expressed by Lao-Tzu, Confucius, Buddha, Pythagoras and Michelangelo, and the great masters of music and art who express the God Force in unique ways. You have the same abilities but you now live in a world that says you are nothing and says that the World controls everything you do, that God is a wrathful God. You are told that if you do not repeat this or that creed, if you do not go to a house of worship and bow your head before certain images, God will not look favourably on you.

You are the God Force. The Nazarene said that you will find the Father within you. Lao-Tzu and Buddha said that you can find the Tao and the Four-Fold Path within yourself. It is within your power. A plant lives and creates the beauty not only of its coloured leaves, but also the budding of a flower that then receives the bee and butterfly. The flower receives the same warming Sun as you do, and produces for a brief time, a beauty your eyes can see, and, if you are in tune, your ears can also hear. This is the God Force at work in a plant, but the God Force is working through you too. You are a flower of this world, expressing itself and budding. But you, unlike the flower, possess a brain and consciousness behind that flower.

You reincarnate onto this plane as a blank canvas, through a parentage that establishes your basis. Because a karmic aspect is required, you are usually incarnated into a family who might say, "You live in a cruel world." However, if you have the God Force within, nothing is impossible in your life and nothing can control you. There is nothing to tell you whether to do this or when not to do that. Consider the energy and power that lies deep within you, a power that so far, each of you have suppressed under many layers of negative spiritual concrete.

Each day, just one slip in your thoughts, one slip of a word, one incorrect action or an incorrect movement of the body and you find yourself denying your divinity. It is true: *You are the God Force*. Some will say that this is heresy and that God is some place 'out there', controlling the world. God *is* out there, but is also within *you*, waiting for outward expression, beyond any personality difficulties that you may have developed during this life. Trying to express yourself, but being born into a family that says, "What you are doing is wrong, you should feel guilt for doing this," *that* is the sin.

Old Chinese sees no 'sin'. It is a word that should not exist. There is nothing in your world that is sin. Whichever church, religion or creed you come from, these places are an aid to the evolution of the individual. And so, Christianity, Buddhism, Taoism, Confucianism, Shinto or Islam can be important for an individual's development. Without them it can be hard to identify the God Force within yourself. How can you claim your divinity, immortality and universality? How can this be brought forth? By refusing to let your world control and align you with the negativity that it currently does. That is a sin. "I have made a great mistake"…*But there are no mistakes*. "I have had an accident"…*But there are no accidents*. The issue is that you are not in tune. "I will do it tomorrow"…*But you delay again*. "I am sick"…*But you are not sick*. Your body may merely be showing deficiencies of your inner self controlling the outer you, but you are never really sick. "I am sick and tired"…*But your higher self is never sick or tired*. "I have a pain in my right leg"...*Your right leg reminds you to work on your spiritual strength.* "I am fat"...*You have misplaced nutrition on your body.*

Such utterances express the control of your subconscious and physical body over your higher energy. Your thought forms seem always to tend toward the negative, toward the undoing of what you are and what you should not be. In Old China it was easy to centre an individual on the positive element of life. By showing him that as he stimulated his life spiritually, he could lift himself out of it, seeing and feeling only Peace.

"I have great loneliness," you may say. Those with inner loneliness deny their divinity for they are, in fact, never alone. Loneliness stems from the subconscious mind, which recalls your parents and friends from your younger years, saying that if you do not have someone else around you physically, reacting to you, then you are lonely. Loneliness cannot be alleviated with the presence of someone else. It must be met by your spirituality or the energy that lies beyond the subconscious. When it has been met you will find yourself – a unique, creative, individual expressing the God Force and nothing will stand in your way. The stronger you express the God Force the more peace there is around you. The more positivity you affirm each day, the more strength and ability you gain to see beyond the horizon, over vast distances, instead of staying mired in the spiritual swamp that so many people find themselves in.

"But, Old Chinese," you say, "It is so easy to talk of this, but harder to do." Consider this: most of your communications, your news and media, are full of death, murder, rape, and terrible difficulties in the world. What if you picked up a newspaper and you could say "Interesting review of a way a person met their probability pattern due to thought," not that you were living in terrible times? Convince enough people in that inflation is unavoidable, you will have mass inflation. Convince enough people that crime is running rampant, then eventually crime will indeed run rampant.

Your civilisation is no different to the civilisations of Rome, Greece and Egypt at their highest points. The only difference is your communication system which is more intricate and advanced, more aimed at expressing negativity. You will hear someone say, "I have a sad story to tell you. Did you hear of Ching Li who was walking down the street, turned the corner and was hit by a heard of water buffalo being chased by a tiger?" And you say "Isn't that sad, poor Ching Li, what will his family do?" His family hopes that they will not turn a corner with wild water buffalo stampeding in the streets. But if Ching Li had been in tune with his God Force, he would not have turned that corner, walking along saying, "Woe is me, my masters control me, I am controlled by society I have no money, I am poor."

If Old Chinese could delete any words from your vocabulary, he would strike out: poor, sick, accident and mistake. It is important that you understand this about negative attitudes: if you think of sickness, it enters your subconscious, thence into your conscious mind. From there it is released into your entire system through hormones and ductless glands, secretions your body has felt before, so even if you were not sick before, your thoughts will dictate that you are now.

You must understand the importance of creating positive inner thought patterns, replacing negativity with positive elements. When you think: I am sick, you must say *"I am positive and well.*" When your head starts to ache, you must say to yourself "*My mind is clear, my energy flows freely. I must breathe deeply and see deep within myself.*" Should your limbs ache, and your body feel weary, do not say "*My body is falling apart.*" Instead, affirm that "*I am a strong, powerful, positive individual.*" If instead you say "*This muscle is giving me pain, I am not in tune,*" you are projecting a negative thought pattern. If you say to yourself "My leg and foot hurt," your subconscious recalls every time in the past that your leg and foot hurt, and so your pain increases. When these painful sensations begin, assert that your leg has good circulation, that you are powerful individual in control of your body, relax and you will soon find through positive visualisation that your body and pain can be controlled by thought. Just as thought can cause the body to weaken, so it can tranquillise and heal.

So what are you saying? That you have no money, you are poor, that you have no control over your life? That the official whom you elected is a terrible person? The country is in great difficulty, but it does not need your negative attitude to add to those difficulties. If you say, "I see only good where I am," you will then see good in those around you and in your situation. Old Chinese once pointed out that if you go out and buy a pink dress or a purple shirt with yellow stripes, as you walk through town you will see more pink dresses or purple shirts with yellow stripes than you could ever imagine. You have placed yourself in a state of observant consciousness. That is the same place in which you should place yourself with regard to negativity. If you say there are too many policemen, you will see nothing but police around you. If you say your world is full of delinquents, then you will have more delinquents around you.

You are what you think and what you attract to yourself in this life. You cannot look at other people or cultures and say they are wrong, for they are what they think and where evolution has taken them. Those steeped in the Catholic, Muslim or Buddhist traditions see things from their perspective. But you have the ability to rise above and go beyond, to travel to ethereal heights of spirituality by seeing and expressing only the positive. At times, no doubt, you will say, "But that person exhibits nothing but negativity." The fact that you can see only that in a person means you must work on it. Eventually you will find that you will see only flowers, not garbage.

The God Force inside you is an expression of power and energy. Bring it forth, don't suppress it. The Nazarene in the garden of Gethsemane said that everyone spoke to the subconscious, but the God Force knew what had to be done. You talk daily to your subconscious mind saying, "Get me out of this situation." If you think you are in this situation, you will be. Stop this, by rising in the morning and saying, "I am a powerful, positive individual. This is a beautiful morning and during it I will be strong and strengthened, all that I see will have beauty, so be it." When you being to feel sickness or a difficulty in your body say, "I am a powerful positive individual, my muscles are strong and my body is beautiful. Everything within it reacts to positivity." Slowly, as you replace the negative thoughts, environments, feelings and projections, your body will come under your control.

It is possible, and Old Chinese says this cautiously, but from the time you are small you are told, "If you eat that you will get fat, or that is fattening." Old Chinese could tell you that for every glass of water you drank, you would gain a pound. I am slim, and at the weight I need to function. Anything that enters my body that is not for this purpose leaves. Say that for everything you eat, truly believing in it, and you will lose weight. But you must remember and you must believe. If you don't, when you eat something and you say, "I wonder if this will make me fat," you will indeed get fat. Old Chinese does not teach this in nutrition, for most people do not want to try the easiest way, they want to try the hardest way.

Now, look at yourself. Is the God Force emanating from you in a surge of light, as if from a pinhole, or just a twinkle once in a while? Do you search through the depths of darkness looking for that light? Your day can bring beauty, even in the face of degradation. By feeling powerful and positive yourself, no matter what is thrown at you, it will be repelled. The stronger you bolster the God Force within you, the more peaceful and powerful you become.

How much peace is around you? Peace. You may ask your questions.

Q: What's the best way to bring out the God Force?

OC: By seeing only positivity and affirming it. You must first clear the field, taking away all the detritus, so that when the God Force comes, you will see the beauty.

Affirm, knowing that you are in control, knowing that you'll always have the money you need and never doubting, but *knowing* that your body is in good shape and condition. Knowing that your energy is power. We will show you the potency of this through an experiment using the Vehicle for a period of 3 to 4 of your weeks. We will affirm what is in his mind and also make affirmations regarding body condition, and while eating regularly, he will lose weight. By strong affirmations you will progress. You are in control, nobody else is. The God Force only emerges when there are positive elements around you, not negativity. Bear in mind that the Living Spirit does not recognise negativity, such as famine, poverty, or war. It does recognise the positive – the beauty of things, which you will evoke when you begin your affirmations. You will see the God Force come forward and the negative elements will fall away from you. Like speckles of sand on a beach, you will walk upon them and never see them. Peace.

Q: If we have complete control of our lives, when does the Law of Karma apply?

OC: When you let it. The nation and era into which you are reincarnated forms approximately 5% of your experience. International or external forces forms around 5%. The people that you meet every day are about 10% of your experience and immediate karma is about 80% of your experience. If you step off the curb into the road, breaking 92 bones in your foot – you are not in tune and you would not have done this. In the case of personal karma, if a person came into your life and they throw a stone at you and hit your head, that is not personal karma that, again, is you not being in tune when that person enters your life. By understanding past relationships you can understand people's reactions to each other. By being in tune and affirming the God Force you can step above 80% of your karma by being at peace with yourself and the nation you live in. You feel at peace and all who surround you will feel peace. Only negativity can drag you down within the karmic cycle. Peace.

Q: My daughter would like to know that if she eats any sugar, not only will it not be harmful, but I think she could believe it would do her good. Can you comment on this?

OC: Firstly, we would have to re-assert that it does good. She brushes her teeth to remove sugar, and at school they teach that sugar is bad. If her teacher said her teeth would fall out if she drank milk, and she truly believed that, then her teeth would indeed fall out. She is still highly susceptible to authority patterns. So it is difficult to place this in her life now, but you could allow her to see what sugar does to the body. You can eat sand and nothing will happen to you. It will cause a little difficulty in the intestines after a while, if you eat it too much. Sugar is like eating sand in a nutritional sense. There are no nutrients in sugar, nor in salt. Other foods contain nutrients. However, you could try saying to a child, "that sugar is bitter" and eventually anything sweet would taste bitter and vice versa. Taste-buds and glands are formed early in a child's development in response to what the mother feeds the child. As you would say to a child, "hot", so you would say the same regarding "bitter." Peace.

Q: Can the cycle of reincarnation ever be broken if we step above it with our will?

OC: No, your will is your mind and your mind is a creation of the subconscious. If you say I want this, I *will* it to happen, then you are merely being stubborn. Exercising your will is painting your bridges as you cross them. Faith is burning them. Do, you cannot will it. Peace.

Q: Is it good karma, doing good deeds and helping people in trouble?

OC: But who is in trouble? You are making a judgement that they are unhappy. Who are you to say anyone is unhappy for you cannot make that judgement. Just as you cannot judge a person who murders someone because of what karma that person attracted to them to be murdered. If someone is sick or sad, that is their spiritual perception at that time. You have no right to infringe upon it. Observe and be aware that they are the same as a person who has spiritual belief. Whether they are Catholic, Protestant or Muslim, where they are is their perception. You would not go to a Muslim and say "You are sick because of what you think." You are not your brother's keeper, you never will or should be so. You are your own keeper first. Love yourself, express the god Force through yourself and your brothers will come to you for the energy and the power you are. The Nazarene never set out to proselytise. He walked the path and people came to see him for what he was. Lao-Tzu sat and taught people that came to him. He did not advertise, nor did he say you needed money to escape poverty, yet he brought people to him. Your world, all too often, seeks to preach and convert others when they cannot effect the changes they believe in on themselves. If you have internal peace you will draw others to you. If the Vehicle walks down the street and in an auric view sees a person riddled with cancer, he cannot tell that person. For that would be an infringement on that person's spiritual evolution, unless that person asks him to. Peace.

Q: What about animals? What if I were to work for the Society for the Prevention of Cruelty to Animals?

OC: An animal will be drawn to man. Each animal is born with a group soul. All man has to do is show it some concern, to feed and care for it. The group soul will sever from that animal and it becomes an individual soul. You might experiment on the animal, you could cause the animal to have great physical pain, but if there is love, the soul evolves. It is only when Man captures and animal in the wild, tames it, then sets it free that the group soul returns. What is cruelty to anything? If you see peace in yourself, you will never see cruelty to animals. Peace.

Q: How did we come to Old Chinese's teachings?

OC: Each of you have been with Vehicle in another lifetime. Each of you had a personal karmic tie, and so the vibration was sent out. You guides asked Old Chinese to return to this part of the world. And so, through sometimes very limited communication with you, the way was opened. You were pulled by someone else, through a word here or there. There was no advertisement saying this was the place to come, yet you came here out of curiosity. But your guide got you here. Peace.

Q: What kind of relationship do we have with our Guides?

OC: Any kind that you want and will allow. What kind of relationship do you have with the person sitting next to you? Are you communicating with them? Do you know their name? Have you talked to them after so many weeks here? You communicate with your Guide. It can be as a distant relative or a friend that you have seen once or twice, or as an unseen force that sometimes manhandles you through life or a companion who gives directions, gives you lessons and teachings, and allows the way to be open for you to see Completeness and not just what is seen with your eyes. That is dependent on how positively you see yourself. Peace.

Q: To communicate with your Guide, must you do it verbally, or will the guide assimilate what you wish to communicate?

OC: You can do it either way, verbally or via thought. You can yell and scream, or whatever fits and feels good for you. Often through verbal communication, because yours is a verbal world, but thoughts are picked up, and every thought becomes reality. Peace.

Q: Do you generally have just one Guide?

OC: You have one librarian or keeper of the gate. That Guide can pull in others around them to help, but there is always only one in charge. Peace.

Q: Who or what is your Guide?

OC: Your Guide has had one past lifetime with you and is no longer in the reincarnation cycle of your Earth. They have gone beyond the Earthly plane, yet return to give guidance and aid to you in your evolution of the physical plane. They are learning from this experience also. Peace.

Q: Are the Guides voluntarily helping us or is that part of their karma?

OC: There is only karma in your world. The Guide volunteers to be your Guide. As to their evolution, in the same way that you have all volunteered to come to this group, so too have the Guides volunteered. But your Guide also has a teacher who explains various karmic patterns. Peace.

Q: I know I'm very earthly and unevolved…

OC: You must get rid of that thought.

Q: But here's the problem…

OC: There are no problems.

Q: But with me, my brother, who was very dear and close to the whole family died, well, committed suicide during a schizophrenic episode. Now all I care about is, that when I die, to be with him and when the rest of my family dies, for all of us to be together…

OC: Why? What if your brother has the opportunity to evolve spiritually, but your thoughts say, "No, I don't want you to, I want you to meet me when I come over." Are you going to project those thoughts and keep him where he cannot develop and grow? Do you want that?

Q: I want him to be happy.

OC: You would want him to evolve if the opportunity arose, but if you say "I want to be together with you when the time comes", you are not helping him evolve. You want your whole family to be together…Are you sure? You are looking at that now, but what of twenty years from now? Imagine: you will all come together. There will be no bodies. You will be able to recognise each other through ethereality. Your ethereal body will be perfect and you'll see individuals as they were. But let us look at an example: If you were in a life with Old Chinese and you came into the spirit world and you said, "I want to see Old Chinese," Old Chinese would slip into the mantle of his lifetime in China – not his real self – but the manifestation that you have visualised. After that brief moment, he would have to return to his Higher Self. The spirit world is continuing spiritual growth and there is no death. We taught at the beginning of this lesson that there is no death. Old Chinese does not see one dead thing. Now, your brother is growing, progressing and he has the potential to learn and work with other people who have committed suicide. In thirty years his spirit will be beyond ethereality, beyond what you are now and will be then.

Visualising your meeting with him when you enter the spirit world, and all being together, you will see him as he passed, but then he will have to leave to continue his evolution. Realise that things do not stay still, for tomorrow you will be different than you are now, and you are different now than you were yesterday. If you understand that, when you reach the spirit world, you will have no difficulty in assimilating and working within what is there. Happiness here will allow evolution to where he is. But, you say, I want to be where my brother is, and Old Chinese offers me the ability to grow beyond where your brother was when he was here. Over the next thirty years you will spiritually unfold. You could pass into the spirit world and progress beyond the spiritual evolution of your brother. But because you wanted to see this, you will stay there, see them and be with them, but you cannot stay there. You must progress. Project your energy and say, "May the spirit of this individual grow continuously and positively." You will then find that when you return to the spirit world that there will be communication but there will be a vibration beyond your imagination now. Peace.

Q: What does positive energy feel like?

OC: Like when you feel good. Positive energy is refreshing and warming. Positive energy, like a refreshing shower after a hot day, is the love you feel, like gentle caresses on your body. This is positive energy. It is when you respond and when the response feels good. Peace.

Q: Why do we need body discipline?

OC: It is not a discipline, it is an experience. As a child must learn mathematics and reading in this lifetime, you must go through a series of lives to gain spiritual understanding within the physical experience. It is a building block in this series of existences you are going through. It is necessary for the next step, like a great ladder, without which you cannot reach the next level and the physical experience is a part of that. In previous existences, before this plane, your existences dealt with other experiences. For now, the physical is a learning process that you have created. Peace.

Q: On average, how many lifetimes do we usually have?

OC: You are a part of two. Before you reincarnate into the earthly plane, your Higher Self splits and reincarnates the first existence, a positive and a negative force, male – female. Over a series of lifetimes you can meet this person as brother, sister, enemy – but very seldom as husband and wife. However, when this happens it is called 'Dual Mate', a challenging experience, for how would you like to live with yourself? That is hard. Your world looks at such a union as the ideal, but it is actually the hardest…And so, each separate, split individual has approximately 9 – 12 lifetimes, so in total, approximately 18 – 24 lifetimes. Peace.

Q: Sometimes there are things that should make us feel bad, but actually make us feel good. Like certain guilt feelings about something that isn't really negative.

OC: Affirm if you have what you call guilt, or if you say, "I should not have done that to a person," if you say, "What I have done is for my highest good and what I have done will allow this person to grow," your perspective will change. But if you say, "What I have done will harm," that thought will go out and it will harm

Q: What should I do if someone I really want to respect me, or someone I love, says something that hurts me?

OC: If someone says that you are as ugly as a water buffalo with warts, that is only their perspective. You cannot be concerned with their myopic deficiencies. Understand that when one person's reality is different than yours, when they say "You're ugly, or "You're bad," what they are really saying is that what you appear to be, is what they are not. Your ugliness from their perspective you, in someone else's view be as beautiful as the rose. If you understand that when someone makes an observation, it is only *their* observation. When you take it as that, it is not personal. Then you will begin to see you are the God Force and what you are is what you feel, not what someone else says you are. Lao-Tzu went for a walk one day and a robber saw him and said, "There goes a cunning man, for he tells no-one what he thinks." A student said of him, "There goes a spiritual man, for he is what he teaches." The emperor said, "There goes a man I cannot trust, for he has peace." Lao-Tzu said, "I am at one with self and I am peaceful no matter what someone thinks of me." If someone says you are ugly and you feel hurt, then what you are saying is that you want to be what they say you are. If someone says that you are ugly, you should reply "My ugliness is beautiful." Peace.

Q: The majority of people do not step out of probability patterns because they are not in tune. They're difficult to step out of, is that correct?

OC: Peace.

Q: How do you feel about the drugs that we use today to alter the mind and body? Do we focus too much on all these drugs and why don't more people think about nutrition and mental processes to cure yourself without the drugs?

OC: Your society says take this pill and you will be well, and so you take that pill and you are well. But that pill causes something else to become unbalanced, so you must take another pill to be well. Artificial or synthetic stimulus of the body shows an individual whose body controls their life, not the individual. It is one of the spiritual evolutions that everyone experiences. The reason it seems highlighted now is because you see it so obviously in mass communication. In Old China there were more drugs used than you have in your whole country, in one year. But you never heard about it. It is part of the physical experience – one that you must step through, a lesson to be learned. Old Chinese is not against those who take drugs, but not for them either. He understands what effect it has on their ethereality and sees the pain they endure. The spirit within grows and this is what Old Chinese examines.

Q: What about the drugs that are used for childbirth? Do you prefer natural childbirth?

OC: Again, whatever you want to do, do it. That is your evolution. Old Chinese looks at the individual. The more natural you can be, the better, but Old Chinese does not say that you taking this drug to help deliver a baby is wrong. For that is where that individual is. However, if you want to experience a higher evolution and be more in tune, then bring it forth naturally, through correct nutrition and bodily exercise. That is like Old Chinese teaching you and another group on the other side of the world that is being taught to kill amoeba and eat them. Two different perspectives – neither of them wrong. Peace.

Q: I belong to a group and I would like very much to tell them what I believe in terms of reincarnation and so forth, but I have held back. Should I?

OC: Sometimes what you are should be felt and not said. If they being to ask, feed them slowly, do not bloat them. Nor should you volunteer it, because just by being what you are, they will be interested. By what you are, they will be excited. Peace.

~ ~ ~ ~ ~ ~ ~ ~ ~

In Old China, there was a sage sitting under a plum tree and the student said to the sage, "I have just come from the Imperial City and I have seen nothing but robberies, I have seen nothing but negativity. I have seen children being beaten. I have seen war. I have seen famine. Within the emperor's palace I saw the emperor put many people to death. I saw rubbish on the street. I saw nothing but terribleness. What should I do?" The sage said, "Come sit with me." And they sat for a while. The sage finally rose and aid, "Come with me." And as they walked they saw the beauty of the flowers, the strength of the trees. They came to a village at the noon hour. People were relaxing and it was a clam time. As they walked through the village, people nodded and spoke. The student said, "But this morning, they were yelling and fighting, they were beating one another," and onward they walked, eventually arriving at a military camp, with soldiers at ease. The student said, "But this morning they were preparing for combat and going to war, now they are relaxing." In the early morning of the next day, the sage and his student arrived at the Imperial City, walking through clean city streets in the fresh morning air. The inhabitants said 'Hello' as they woke with the day. They came to the Imperial palace and walked in, sitting down and the emperor emerged and said, "Today is the day of peace and love. Each person who comes to me this day, I give a part of myself to. Today hold nothing but positivity towards my people." That evening they left the palace and the student said, "But yesterday there was nothing but death." The teacher turned and said, "What you are is what is around you. What you are is what you'll see. What you are is where you will be."

May the Living Spirit that is in all life come forward and give each of you Peace.

~ Whatever the problem seems to be, the solution already exists ~

SUBCONSCIOUS MIND

London – 18 February 1975

Blessings and Peace to you all. May the beauty that comes forth from the inner recesses of your imagination come forward in the beauty of life, in the life that you create each day. Peace.

In Old China, an emperor was standing on a very high hill, his great army spread throughout the valley below. He had an intricate system of commands for communicating orders to his generals and officers. He could see where the battles were to be fought, and where the other armies were positioned. When the battle began, the emperor would signal to the right and the right would attack. He would signal to the left and the left would attack. He would signal to the middle and it would attack and then with another signal, it would retreat and then attack again. The battle went on for hours and soon the emperor saw a weakness and he sent his troops into that area and they eventually overcame their opponents.

In essence, this is analogous of your conscious and subconscious mind: you are the emperor and your subconscious, the army, does not see what is going on, solely reliant on the demands of the conscious mind, directing it, recording everything that consciousness sends to it, whether it is through hearing, sound, colour, taste, or touch. It goes blindly here and there, working on demand. Everything that is put into it, it will do. If the conscious self says, "Go this way", and the subconscious begins to go and has never been there before, either in thought, or in action, the way will be very hard.

Let us look in a little more detail at what your subconscious is. When you reincarnated into the body that you are now, your subconscious was new, a clean slate, a new book that you begin to write upon. Your five senses become the pen with which your book is written in this lifetime. Everything in which your senses partake goes into your book. Upon the separation of the body and the soul, the book goes to your Higher Self, or to the spiritual library that is your Higher Self. But, in most lifetimes, individuals react and work because of what the subconscious mind presents. The subconscious mind records everything that you feel, see, hear, touch or taste –

even those things that merely glimmer on the periphery of your senses, or that go on in the distant background – it records them and it makes a note of them. Let us say that you are the general in an army, you are the subconscious. Let us say that your emperor says, "Attack to the left" and you go to the edge of a deep ravine. Then you recall that during the last attack to the left you met an opposing army in the ravine, so that when you come to that ravine again, you retreat, even though there the enemy army is not actually there.

You may think you have certain likes and dislikes, perhaps saying to yourself, I do not like asparagus and it will go into your subconscious, or someone will say asparagus is not good for you and because you rely upon them, you believe that they are telling the truth, it records. And then, in a group of vegetables mixed together, you eat asparagus. It goes into your stomach, there is a reaction with the nerve endings and the subconscious mind goes back to the point where it said you do not like asparagus, it is not good for you. So, even though you were not aware of eating it, you will get an upset stomach. Everything that is in your subconscious, you are responsible for, for you have put it there. You chose the parentage that you reincarnated through, selecting them because of what they would place in your subconscious through education and teaching. "Make sure that before you go out into the cold, put on your coat, or you will catch the flu". And so children do this each and every day.

When they have grown up, away from their parents, they walk outdoors and it is a beautiful day. They walk down a path and someone says, "It is a cold day," and the subconscious mind says. "Cold days bring on the flu" so they begin to feel ill because they do not have their coat.

Ninety eight percent of your lives are run on subconscious projection and instant replay of what has been placed there before. It is very important to realise that individuals become enslaved to what they have placed within themselves. There are negatives in your world that do not allow you to grow. "I will do that" is negative, because you are putting it off until tomorrow. The subconscious mind says, "He will do that sometime". There are other negatives that you use, let us say that when you were small, your mother said, "You are bad, and because you are bad, you must go to your room and see no one". Now, when you are working in business and someone says to you, "That was a bad thing you did," the subconscious says, "Bad" – "Isolation" and you become fearful and you say, "I must be alone, I must run away, I must escape".

Psychotherapists and psychologists say that you must delve deep into the subconscious to retrieve such experiences and get them out in the open. What good would that do? In order to understand why you catch a cold on a hot summer's day when someone says "Isn't it cold?" But what do you do about it? Do you laugh or do you get another cold? The subconscious mind is very subtle and intricate, working through suggestions from others, through feelings, especially of those people whose opinions you respect. If you have faith in their words, it becomes indelible.

Thus you become a slave to the things that lie within you, a slave to bad health, poverty, having other people move and push you where they want you to go, rather than where you feel you should be. Most people in your world never get beyond the subconscious mind, regardless of whichever religion they follow, never get beyond the subconscious mind or recognise that there is a Higher Self. They say that if you do this or that, it is a sin, and sin is punishable by death, or hell. And so, the mind takes these things on and you commit what your world moralistically says, "Is a sin." You feel that you are going to hell and because it has been buried deep within you mind since early childhood, you feel that your life if no longer worth anything and you will find yourself in the gutter.

Old Chinese, in all the teachings and places that he has been, through the Vehicles of your world, has not found many who know how to go beyond the subconscious mind and allow their inspirational spiritual self to come through. Most of your world works on the psychic perception, or the projections of the subconscious, the psychological and psychotherapeutic areas. The reason that you hit your wife is not because you hated your mother; the reason that you dislike this or that, is not because you have sexual tendencies that will cause great difficulty. Everything that you have received in your first thirteen years, you knew was going to be put there. Before reincarnation, your Higher Self, along with the Guide who works with you through most of your lifetime, chooses your parentage, the genetic, national and international factors, chooses the parents for their personal and interpersonal relationships, and pulls all those aspects together allowing the reincarnation to take place. So the inter-reactions that happen – divorce, separation, death, feelings, life and longevity are already foreseen in the first thirteen years, with perhaps one or two exceptions every 100 years. The traits and experiences that you gain through your parental pattern are not necessarily instrumental in subconsciously establishing what you are, since that was already known, it is merely balancing it. It is from the age of thirteen that you begin to use what has been placed there and what you need. If you had been born a thirteen year old, you would be born with idiosyncrasies or difficulties that were placed there during that time for you to experience later in the rest of your life. However, since the female body is not capable of gestating a thirteen year old, there is a latent spiritual understanding of things, established patterns that will allow the individual to begin work upon his life at thirteen.

Between the ages of thirteen and eighteen, you start to see what you have created. Those years will mark you and you will say, "Oh, the teen years are terrible, the worst years of my life." The reason you say this is because you are looking at yourself. Children are the result of programming placed within them, or allowed to be placed within them, and thus, you see yourself. Those who are orphaned and have not been influenced by parents are marked by the experiences they go through.

Now, each of you have the ability to relax the subconscious, to re-programme it. If you are receptive to the energy of the Higher Self, you no longer need to rely on cheap spiritual experiences that have a tendency to nag and egg you on because they reek of the subconscious mind. Very few people in your world understand the Higher Self coming into your life, because most of them allow it to come through the subconscious, and that is like walking through a forest of cane, blindfolded and not hitting a tree. When you entered the forest, you were healthy and strong, but when you leave it, you will be battered and bruised. No longer with the same thought forms, nor the same energy force.

Those who say that things must be proven and thought out, that things must have a logical end are focusing their entire projection on the subconscious. More people in your world relate and worship subconscious projections than those who allow the higher essence of the God Force to permeate them, which would enlighten and beautify their life. The holy men of your world say, "If you do not do that, you will go to Hell," or "You will not receive goodness." It is interesting that none of the great masters said things like that, only their followers who wanted to instil fear in people, because they did not have the charisma of the master. The only reason Paul projected so many rules and regulations, so many do's and do not's, is because he lacked the charisma of the Nazarene, instead having to instil fear in others so that they would follow Christian precepts. There has never been an accurate account of the true teachings of the masters, whether it be Lao-Tzu, Buddha, Confucius, Pythagoras or Zoroaster. All you have are many people trying to project what they believe these masters were and what went on. That is why Old Chinese feels it is important for the individual to contact the God Force within themselves, so they do not need to rely upon a system, or a pattern. They should develop that pattern inside themselves, finding the divinity, universality, immortality and eternity that is within.

How many times have you settled down to meditate and in the meditation itself, you have thought of what you did yesterday, what you hope to do tomorrow, what someone said to you three years ago, the colour of the new vehicle you will buy in four and a half years? And you then say to yourself, "I cannot meditate, thoughts run in and out of my mind". The subconscious mind is like that; if the emperor does not exercise or deploy his troops, they will grumble, moving and milling about. They do not like to be relaxed and at rest. The only time they are relaxed is when he is exercising them, teaching them, or focussing them on a specific task. That is the way to relax and re-programme your subconscious. The emperor cannot tell his assembled troops that the next time they come to a valley and they do not retreat, that won't mean there are soldiers in the valley. Even though it has happened before, he puts them through the exercise and when they get to the valley they discover there is nothing there. He replaces the conditioning with another form of conditioning.

And so, the things that cause you loss, hardship, physical pain and agony, the things that make you seek a religion, philosophy, faith or creed are programmed elements within your subconscious, making you reliant on certain things. A man you respect can say, "If you do not do this, you will not have a good life," and you will not have a good life. Your parental pattern might say, "You are not musical, so do not even try," and you will not have a bit of music in your life.

So what to do with this monster you have lying deep within yourself, in the area of the pineal gland? How to begin to utilise it in strength for betterment of life and to not be subjected by it? Old Chinese has seen many who walk down the street, enjoying the flowers and trees, and someone sitting beside the way says, "It is a bad day," and the consciousness doesn't catch that, but the subconscious picks it up. And so, the next bird they see, the subconscious says, "It is a bad day," and the person says, "I hate birds." It is a very thin line, but you are here to step upward, learn to utilise it and go beyond it. Now, how do you do it? You do it the way the emperor did with his soldiers. You keep it busy while you re-programme it. Let us say that you are worried about certain happenings in your life. You take the subconscious mind and you visualise those happenings, or see yourself doing something within them. You breathe in and you exhale, you breathe in the happening and then you exhale it. You breathe in and you say, "I am in control of this situation and I will always be in control."

Slowly, the subconscious mind replaces the old programming with a new one that says, "This individual is in control, he will jump into the valley, even though it is filled with forty thousand troops armed with swords, but because of his determination, he will probably be able to walk above the valley, instead of jumping into it." It is only by replacing fear, by replacing the negativity and by systematically working with the subconscious that you begin to bring forth the Higher Self.

If you are getting energy from the Higher Self, it will not record on the subconscious mind. There will be those who say, "I had a high religious experience, I walked with the masters and the spiritual energy." They had sensory orgasms of their subconscious minds, they tasted every taste they had every tasted, they smelled every smell they had ever smelled, they are ravished by their own perceptions. What comes from the Higher Self is recorded on the subconscious mind, meaning you want it recorded there because you want to see the good works you have done, but the Higher Self, or God Force, is a pure projection, not one that relies on proving oneself. Be cautious of those who say they are great healers, or great teachers, for a teacher will not know what he is teaching, a healer will not know what he is healing, a Vehicle will not remember what he has conveyed. If they did, it would mean that the communication, the energy force was going through their subconscious mind, and like the entity that walked blindfolded into a forest of cane, it would come out black and blue and you would not recognise it. So – the Higher Self does not record. It is like standing on a mountain and as you stand there the wind gusts around you and you feel the wind but do not see it. You do not grasp it, you only feel the wind around you, and it goes and refreshed others. The same applies to the Higher Self, you will have a feeling of it as it goes around the subconscious, but you will not see it, you will not be able to identify it, but you will know that it is working.

You have been told that the Nazarene was baptized by John who said, "Come and enter," not recognising him. He pushed him under the water and the soul, or subconscious, of the Nazarene died and went back to the Higher Self. When the Nazarene came forward, John recognised him, for he did not look upon an individual who was scarred by a subconscious mind. He was looking at an individual who had a direct connection to the Higher Self, to all the energy of cosmic forces. He saw a man who did not fool around with subconscious projection.

In essence, your entire role in this lifetime is not to record anything in your subconscious mind at all. But you have not yet reached that stage, but we will work with helping you understand how to go one step beyond. Let us visualise that you are dealing with a person in your work that is causing you trial and tribulation. You have pulled a person into your business whom you believed was going to be an attribute. Then, suddenly, their habits and tendencies being to agitate and irk you. So you sit down and begin to train your subconscious army. You visualise that person, you breathe and pull that person in, you exhale them saying, "This individual (calling the individual by their name) is positive and powerful." Then you breathe in saying, "I am in control of all situations around me." The subconscious relaxes and centres itself. The Higher Self: like the breeze that embraces you. As it wraps around you it picks up the sensory accent of that individual and a pure energy goes forth and surrounds the individual. When you come out of your relaxation you are not aware of anything having happened. In fact, you will say, "I do not feel any different." But the person who has been projected has a different feeling. Doing that each and every day, the person will be so inflamed with positivity, that as the two of you come together daily, you will see the difference within them.

The subconscious mind is what you are right now, the Higher Self being what you can both project and pull to you. All your subconscious minds are working right now. The Higher Self is glittering and filtering through, like a sieve full of salt, but as you learn to relax that subconscious, the Higher Self will work more and more. It is hard to be harmonious in your world, so if you encounter a person that says, "Oh, it is so beautiful being spiritual, I find so much energy and strength, I have such great health," try climbing a mountain and watch them work. The more finely in tune you become, the more immune you become to negativity and disease. Your world is full of subconscious personalities and inharmonious people, but as you pull away from them you encounter loneliness and you are like a fish out of water. There is a purpose to using and projecting your Higher Self, as the people pulled toward you will feel immediate harmony. However, there will be times during your journey to finding your Higher Self that you will sometimes wonder, "Wouldn't it be nice to eat some junk food again, like everyone else."

Spiritual development does not put you in a special class. If you feel you are better than another person, you can rest assured that individual is probably better than you. If you are conscious of being better than others, you are experiencing the deluded elation and beauty that the subconscious has a tendency to transmit.

Subconsciously, you can control every aspect of your life, you are the emperor, the captain of your boat, commanding your crew to row even though they cannot see where they are rowing. They follow everything you tell them to do. Spiritual development is the discovery of self. You will not evolve from this plane by following a religion, creed philosophy or guru, but by following your true inner self. By relaxing the subconscious and becoming a projection of the God Force, the Higher Self.

Pythagoras found that, if for the first six years of their tutelage, his students did not speak a word, he was able to re-programme their subconscious in a positive way. He was eliminating one of their least important senses: the verbal. Thus his students re-adjusted what they saw and heard. Someone might say to you, "You look beautiful in blue," then you will say to someone else, "So and so said that I look beautiful in blue." This causes your subconscious to react, telling you that you only look beautiful in blue around that person. Silence in the Pythagorean school allowed a taming of the subconscious and development of the Higher Self. Peace.

You may ask your questions.

Q: Are dreams from the Higher Self?

OC: There are two types that are not, the first type uses everything you have absorbed into your mind, your subconscious or the pineal gland, call it what you will, which allows your mind to release the pressure after a very busy day. In this type of dream you will find yourself walking down a road aged thirty four years old, the road you grew up on when you were five, yet the people you meet were your friends when you were aged nineteen and the great blizzard in your dream happened when you were twenty six. These are random releases of your subconscious, with some negligible symbolism. The second type of dream is a nightmare, caused by too much food or incorrect diet and food combinations. In these nightmares things that you have experienced become gigantic and intensified. Recently, a small boy ate 22 olives before sleeping and dreamt that a wolf ate his favourite dog.

The other type of dream is when the subconscious relaxes and the soul, or Higher Self, projects into it. You may encounter projections of other people sleeping, of those who have passed on, because they inhabit the same realm. If you wake with the feeling that someone you know is ill, it is because you have received that projection during the night. Peace.

Q: Is the limiting of one of the senses helpful?

OC: With discipline, it is helpful, but chaos without it. Pythagoras projected positivity, yet his students didn't see him for three years. He taught them from behind a drawn curtain, all the better to listen and focus on his words. But it must be disciplined, so the answer is yes – with caution. Peace.

Q: Could you explain the caution?

OC: The caution is that if you limit one sense your subconscious will react to that. You should have an experienced person around you who knows what to do should you begin to panic. If you close your eyes and place something over them through which you can see light, you will eventually have the sensation of blindness and you may experience a sense of panic, wanting to rip away whatever is on your eyes in order to see again. Peace.

Q: What part does meditation play in controlling the subconscious?

OC: Usually, meditation is not what many believe to be meditation. Meditation is a discipline, like the emperor training his soldiers. That is meditation, the Higher Self appearing is not meditation, it is a more uplifting and complex experience. Meditation is centering yourself, allowing you to replace negativity with positive energy. But many people say they blank themselves out in order to meditate. There are very few who can do that, but even those who do are gaining no positive experience at all. To be a balanced person you must have a measure of imbalance. You must tread you path moving slowly from side to side, not walking down the middle, for he who walks down the middle of the road will get hit from both directions. Meditation must be a balance, so those who meditate twenty four hours a day are imbalanced. You are in this world to be a part of it, not to escape from it. Peace.

Q: When we have periods of relaxation, should we actually not just physically relax, but relax the subconscious, is that right?

OC: It is through visualisation that the subconscious relaxes. Let us say you are relaxed here, breathing in and exhaling every person in this room. As you breathe them in and release them, the subconscious becomes centred, not dissipated, and the Higher Self is able to move freely. By this method the resulting energy will be projected to these individuals. Peace.

Isn't it curious that there are a group of men in your world that have become authorities in the utilisation of the subconscious mind? What would you think if every person in this room produced an opinion or dogma, presented it to the world and it became systematised? Did you know that the word 'schizophrenia' came from a time when 60% of the vitamins and minerals now known to exist in your food and body were as yet undiscovered? So, if someone says you are schizophrenic say, "I hope so," because if you say you are not, you are.

One further word. Let us say you are dealing with people who come from former lifetimes, how does the subconscious work with this? Your current subconscious has not existed before this life, so when you are with a person from a past life you do not remember this fact. You may have a sense of, "I have seen this person before,", which is the Higher Self projecting through your subconscious, pulling you to each other and there will be a recognition of who you both are. You will remember, you will say, "I know, we were in that lifetime where we dug horses' graves in the north of Sweden." An individual has the ability to nullify and repress what has been before, which is what hypnotism seeks to reveal and unlock. Hypnotism replaces subconscious suggestions with positive suggestions, but it is important that the suggestion is placed in your previous lifetime. If you are trying to stop smoking nicotine, hypnotism will take you back and say, "You will not smoke nicotine again." But should you encounter an adored friend from that time who says, "Smoke with me," you will smoke and that subconscious suggestion will overpower the hypnotic suggestion. If a person can remove themselves from the habit pattern, or difficulty they are facing, positive and harmonious projections can replace the negative projections. Peace.

Q: Is it possible for the present day hypnotist to regress a person pre-birth and cause them to remember past lives?

OC: There are those who can do it, because of the energy that is around you. They are doing the same thing the emperor did to his troops, engaging them while teaching them. Your subconscious relaxes and you are tapping into the Higher Self, going beyond the subconscious, taking a book off a high spiritual shelf and leafing through it. There should be caution this: when Old Chinese goes to your spiritual library and pulls out the book that contains your time as a bell-ringer at Notre Dame, he does not read only the part where you became deaf because of the sound. The regresser can go to that part of the book and say, "Re-live this day", and you will be deafened. That is a caution. The answer is yes – with a great amount of caution. Peace.

Q: Would it be a generalisation to say that the subconscious works on fears and the Higher Self works on what we call 'Love'?

OC: That is a very close analogy. Again we are dealing with words that elicit different reactions from individuals. Some fear being too rich, did you know? Fear lies dormant in the subconscious until you bring it forward, and your world usually reacts to fear, which brings the fear further forwards. The Higher Self deals with love, for it is impossible for you to truly love each other without the God Force within, which is a projection of the Higher Self, that much is true. Peace.

~~~~~~~~~~

In Old China, a sage sat by the road. Where he sat there were four roads leaving a single lane. A young student came past and, looking at each road, asked the sage, "Which one should I take?" The sage said, "None of them." The student asked, "Why? I must go somewhere." The teacher replied, "If you do not know where you are going, stop, until you know where you are going." And so the student sat by the teacher and another student came and said, "Which way should I go?" Before the teacher could answer, the first student said, "Go the middle way." Then another student arrived and asked, "Which way should I go?", but before the teacher answered, the student said, "Go down the left way." And a third student came by and asked, "Which way should I go?" And the student, before the teacher could come forward said, "Go to the far right way." And another student came by and said, "Which way should I go?" The student replied, "Go to the way next to the right." And eventually the first student returned, bloody and beaten. The second student returned without any clothes. The third student did not return. The fourth student returned saying the river had washed out. And the student who had been sitting by the sage jumped up and said with happiness, "I know which way to go, I have been a teacher, I have been a sage, I will go to the far right." Saying that, he ran down the road. The other students who had returned from the other roads were tired and turned to their teacher and asked, "Why did he choose that way?" And the teacher said, "There is no return from death."

May the Living Spirit be with you all. Blessings and Peace.

—